Unleash the Beauty and Power of Love

Imagine what you become when love streams out of you

H. C. VILLANUEVA

WestBow
PRESS

A DIVISION OF THOMAS NELSON

Scripture taken from the New King James Version. Copyright 1979, 1980, 1982 by Thomas Nelson, inc. Used by permission. All rights reserved.

WestBow Press books may be ordered through booksellers or by contacting:

WestBow Press
A Division of Thomas Nelson
1663 Liberty Drive
Bloomington, IN 47403
www.westbowpress.com
1-(866) 928-1240

ISBN: 978-1-4497-3624-8 (sc)
ISBN: 978-1-4497-3625-5 (hc)
ISBN: 978-1-4497-3623-1 (e)

Library of Congress Control Number: 2012903191

Printed in the United States of America

WestBow Press rev. date: 04/27/2012

Contents

To the Reader

Dear friend,

This book invites you on stage and puts a spotlight on you.

As your heart touches the ensuing pages, a probing light shines on the alcove of your soul. You may delight in the life exposed. On the other hand, you may not like what lingers within or what lurks from the past. However, when you embrace the love of God, you move forward to unfold the gift of life.

I extend to you my heartfelt gratitude as you read *Unleash the Beauty and Power of Love*. During the coming days, months, and years, truth unleashes its power, passion shows its zeal, and love unveils its face. In these moments, look above and search within.

Life is to be lived in fullness.

Sadly, many look to alcohol, drugs, fame, power, selfish desire, or tasteless passion to usher in joy, peace, and love. These solutions move us backward. Hate is more caustic, peace is nowhere to be found, and love is tainted beyond recognition. As a result, we move apart and care less for one another.

If we do nothing, then our demise moves closer and our end is certain. However, we can change our world. When more people share a bit of care, love sprouts from the ashes of hate and hope shines through the cloudy plights of mankind.

You have a role to share love to a hurting world. Share your goodness in the open, *Unleash the Beauty and Power of Love*, and see lives transform right before your eyes.

H. C. Villanueva
Honolulu, Hawaii

Dedicated to You

This book is dedicated to you and to anyone who yearns to embrace the fullness of life. As we move forward to discover who we are and why we are here, let us heed Solomon's advice:

> *Whatever your hand finds to do, do it with your might;*
> *for there is no work or device or knowledge or*
> *wisdom in the grave where you are going.*
> *I returned and saw under the sun that--*
>
> *The race is not to the swift,*
> *Nor the battle to the strong,*
> *Nor bread to the wise,*
> *Nor riches to men of understanding,*
> *Nor favor to men of skill;*
> *But time and chance happen to them all.*
>
> *For man also does not know his time:*
> *Like fish taken in a cruel net,*
> *Like birds caught in a snare,*
> *So the sons of men are snared in an evil time,*
> *When it falls suddenly upon them.*
>
> --Ecclesiastes 9:10-12

Unearth the Gift
Introduction to Your Inner Discovery

Love is the music of the soul. Love is a tune from above.

Everyone attempts to sing the melody of heaven. Sadly, we taint our lives, blurt out songs of hate, and hurt each other.

In the furnace of hate, love still exists. However, we have to look harder to find love in us and around us.

In the midst of struggle, we need to stop, be still, and look above.

During quiet times with God, love becomes clearer. With a gentle heart, love grows to bind your senses, your mind, and your being. At the same time, life sings louder when you share love with no strings, no conditions, and no longings in return.

In quiet junctures, hope opens the gate, love unfolds its beauty, and truth reveals its power. Nurture the moments. One fleeting moment may be the rare time the soul opens its door. One instant may be the split second the mind welcomes change. One sobering moment may be the only occasion the heart welcomes love. Unfortunately, many squander their chances and live in a spiritual coma, and as a result, go to their graves with their dreams shackled, their potential unreleased, and their gifts from God unwrapped.

I pray for moments of meekness as you unfold the life you have been given. Also, I pray for openness as you meet the Giver of life. Revere the moments. Nurture the tenderness. *"Redeeming the time..."* (Eph. 5:6).

Each day, unwrap your gift.

Search the richness of heaven planted in your soul. As you seek the One who gave you life, follow the homing beacon God has placed in your heart.

Jesus said, "*I am the way, the truth, and the life*" (John. 14:6a). As you look to God, He will unveil your life, your identity, and your destiny.

Unleash the Beauty and Power of Love directs you to the Bible.

"*All Scripture is given by inspiration of God, and is profitable for doctrine, for reproof, for correction, for instruction in righteousness, that the man of God may be complete, thoroughly equipped for every good work*" (2 Tim. 3:16, 17).

The Bible is the guidebook to instruct the heart, the measuring stick to gauge your life, and the lamp to light your path.[1]

Search the Word of God.[2]

Write the law, the love, and the grace of God on the tablet of your soul.

The Word will guide you, help you, and give you life. However, you decide how deep truth sinks into the inner sanctum of your soul. At the same time, you select the intensity with which love shines from your heart.

Unleash the Beauty and Power of Love has seven sections. They are:

Part One:	Rhythm of Love
Part Two:	Sharing the Heart
Part Three:	Facets of Life
Part Four:	Hearts Grown Cold
Part Five:	Tools of Life
Part Six:	Life Under the Sun
Part Seven:	Your Next Step

Seven principles are woven into this book. These truths provide guidance to souls searching for peace, meaning, and life. These principles are:

1. Love is the currency of life. The heart is the soul's garden where compassion grows.

2. Creation and life are meant to praise God--no other purpose, no other intent.

3. God is the Source of joy, peace, and life.

4. God gave gifts ready to be unwrapped. Open your gift today.

5. Live in the fullness God intended. Even in tough times, glean the moments.

6. The duty of man is *"to fear God and keep His commandments"* (Eccles. 12:13b).

7. Embrace God's love and share it each day.

These truths work. They transformed my life and helped many friends. These principles can change your life, too.

When you bear these truths, you open the gift of life.

Unleash the Beauty and Power of Love exposes the life within.

This book invites you to slow down when you clash with truth and to stop and listen during trying times. At the end each chapter, the *Questions to Search Your Soul* section encourages you to look within. Probing questions prime the heart to expose its essence. Do the exercises. Answer the questions. Be honest. Be open. And be true to yourself.

As you walk forward, find kindred souls. The journey sweetens when noble hearts surround you. Form support groups with family, friends, and neighbors. Share life lessons. Uphold one another in truth, nurture one another in love, and help one another march toward meaningful lives.

"Being confident of this very thing, that He who has begun a good work in you will complete it until the day of Jesus Christ" (Phil. 1:6).

God walks near you and love waits to be ushered in. Each day, foster a teachable heart and nurture a humble spirit. Set aside a soul-searching time to take off your mask, bare your essence, and find your life. As you spend quiet time in solitude, listen to the gentle voice and follow the nudging unction of God.

Be ready to reflect the glory of God. Engage your life for an eternal cause. *Unleash the Beauty and Power of Love.*

Get in the arena. Step on the stage. Have a great drama.

Enjoy your show.

Have a great life.

We Love You

Part One

RHYTHM OF LOVE

1. Ashes to Masterpiece

2. 0% Feeling

3. Love Is ...

4. Two Voices

5. Poem: Just Me, the Voice Crying Within, I

Part One: **Rhythm of Love**

CHECKLIST

Principles to instill

- Love binds feelings within the sacrificial cord of promise.
- Pain is experienced. After the ordeal, beauty unfolds.
- Growth is a sign of life, and change is part of being alive.

Things to do

- Find ways to share love each day.
- Create a loving place for family, friends, and neighbors.
- Walk your faith, live your dreams, and work your plans.

A life to build

- Each day, tell family members you love them.
- Encourage three people every day.
- Share love with family, friends, and neighbors.

1

Ashes to Masterpiece

*To cross the great unknown to harvest
love is a challenge we all face.*

The creature looks ugly.

It detests browsing eyes and turns away passing minds. Yet, this living thing intrigues truth seekers. The caterpillar exists as one of the wonders of nature--a masterpiece of creation.

As a tiny creature, a caterpillar crawls and feasts on juicy leaves. It eats, and eats, and grows.

As it grows, the caterpillar sheds its skin. After molting, it gulps air and stretches its new covering. When the skin dries, and the air has been released, the expanded skin becomes the creature's enlarged fragile shell.

The caterpillar eats, grows bigger, and sheds its skin again. After a while, the caterpillar prepares a cocoon, seals itself inside, and turns into a chrysalis or pupa. Then, nature goes to work by transforming this living thing.

For days, it hangs alone. It is a mystery to behold. In silence, it changes. In solitude, it transforms.

Then, the butterfly greets the world by opening a small hole and begins the work of getting out of the cocoon.

It turns.

It wiggles.

It struggles.

At first, the butterfly is too frail inside the cocoon. However, it builds strength as it twists and squirms inside its protective pouch. Without strained efforts, the butterfly is too weak to fly. Without the struggle, it will die.

After many ordeals, beauty unfolds. A magnificent creature comes out. The butterfly is a splendor to see. It is bright. Beautiful. Pure. Gentle. And majestic.

The creature feels the warmth of the sun, faces the wind, and flaps slowly to dry its moist wings. Then, it flies. It soars. It is free to explore the bounties of creation.

To the caterpillar and every creature with breath, change is a sign of life. Growth is part of being alive.

Pain and hardships prepare a life for the next season of growth.

Grand design

"The heavens declare the glory of God; and the firmament shows His handiwork" (Ps. 19:1).

A dazzling butterfly lives within each caterpillar. Likewise, the image of God is etched in each soul. And there is a dazzling being inside each of us.

"And the LORD God formed man of the dust of the ground, and breathed into his nostrils the breath of life; and man became a living being" (Gen. 2:7).

God's breath gave an eternal spirit to each of us and a masterpiece ingrained within each soul.

This spirit yearns to shout the splendor of God and wants to reach out to heaven.

The love of God shines like as a homing beacon to guide willing souls back to the Creator. As you embrace the love of the God, you shape your life, unveil your purpose, and live with meaning.

You go through ordeals, failures, and triumphs to expose your essence. In the process, a meek soul reveals hope, peace, and love.

Seek your true self.

To do so, pause.

Take time outs to hear God.

When the heart is calm, clarity reveals itself. When the mind is pure, truth unveils its secrets sooner. When the soul is humble, change comes more quickly.

Sadly, competing noises distract the mind, burden the heart, and hamper the soul. Many neglect the heart crying inside. As a result, change comes more slowly and life stays in the dark longer.

Challenges

To cross the great unknown to harvest love is a challenge we all face.

We are all traveling.

We travel toward something.

We journey to find out who we are and what has been placed in our soul.

Each day of passage, you build a life. You face challenges, meet opportunities, and try to find the essence, the meaning, and the purpose of being on earth.

No matter how old you are, life is a work in progress. You unwrap your potential by taking small steps forward and unveil your true self by sharing your life with others.

God is at work to draw from you the bounties of heaven. However, you choose the path and the pace of the journey. You choose what you become and decide how brightly love shines before God and others.

Change depends on how you allow God to work in your heart. Progress depends on how you let God guide you each step of the way.

The Bible says, *"My brethren, count it all joy when you fall into various trials, knowing that the testing of your faith produces patience. But let patience have its perfect work, that you may be perfect and complete, lacking nothing"* (James 1:2-4).

Trials bring out the best in you. Trials also expose the worst aspect of the soul.

Tough times humble the heart and purify the mind. On the other hand, tough times can also harden the mind with pride, lace the soul with regret, and wrap the heart with hate.

During times of struggle, you wonder how life becomes a masterpiece.

During quiet times, search within and look above. You will find materials to make your life a wonder to set eyes on.

God says, *"Behold, I have refined you, but not as silver; I have tested you in the furnace of affliction"* (Isa. 48:10).

Draw near to God *"that Christ may dwell in your hearts through faith; that you being rooted and grounded in love, may be able to comprehend with all the saints what is the width and length and depth and height--to know the love of Christ which passes knowledge; that you may be filled with all the fullness of God. Now to Him who is able to do exceedingly abundantly above all that we ask or think, according to the power that works in us, to Him be glory in the church by Christ Jesus to all generations, forever and ever. Amen"* (Eph. 3:17-21).

Symphony of life

There is a melody in the soul waiting to be sung.

However, we struggle to find the right song for our lives.

We search in desperation to find peace, meaning, purpose, and love. We rummage for temporal things to fill the emptiness inside and blindly follow pride to soothe selfish wants. Most of all, we struggle to search for the One who gave us life.

How about you?

What is the melody in your heart?

What is the rhythm of your soul?

God longs to see your life sing with joy and hear you hum the tune of heaven.

Get a song sheet from above. Write your life music. Sing the melody of love playing in your soul. Keep composing your life because beautiful lyrics are waiting to be written.

Each day, there is a love to be expressed, a promising life to be explored, and an amazing journey at hand.

Step out.

Live so others can enjoy your tune.

Make others smile and love people without conditions, for *". . . if God so loved us, we also ought to love one another"* (1 John. 4:11).

As you journey, keep dreaming, keep marching, and keep singing.

Share the love of God, for it is soothing and transforming. *"There is no fear in love; but perfect love casts out fear, because fear involves torment. But he who fears has not been made perfect in love"* (1 John 4:18).

As you prepare, practice, and persist, life transforms into a masterpiece. You become a gentle song to broken souls and a soothing melody to those living in despair.

Love begins with . . .

Love begins with you, not with others.

Stop chasing after love. Stop looking for love in dark corners of the world. Stop seeking love in people. Stop thinking that love can be found in things. Search within and look above.

Look to God.

Look in your soul.

Is there love?

Sadly, regret taints the love inside. Hurt pulls the heart to despair and hate blurs the mind to the truth. An untamed heart distorts the love you were meant to give, to receive, and to experience.

When you embrace the love of God, you will be able to say, *"For God has not given us a spirit of fear, but of power and of love and of a sound mind"* (2 Tim 1:7).

Love does not require perfection. However, love does require patience, goodness, merit, passion, and humility.

God must be the center of life--no other way. You will not be able to truly love without God. Also, you will not be able to maintain love without God.

There are no easy ways to build a life. There are no magic potions to usher in peace. Furthermore, there are no shortcuts to experience love. It compels sacrifice and demands correct materials.

Life requires the right Builder.

Go to God.

Find out what needs to be restored. He has your life blueprint.

When you look to heaven, you find your bearing. When you give your heart to God, you become a masterpiece beaming with beauty, power, and love.

Chapter 1: **Ashes to Masterpiece**

QUESTIONS TO SEARCH YOUR SOUL

A. What holds you back from becoming a masterpiece?

Fear? Pride? Hurt? Failure? Your past?
Search your soul.
Find the answers.

B. Daily life: *Unleash the Beauty and Power of Love* to your family

Read 1 Corinthians 13. (See Appendix II.)
Create a loving place for family members.
Each day, tell family members you love them.

C. Self-discovery

Be mindful that grating people and tough times help you grow.
Find three people willing to grow with you.
Read one Bible chapter out loud each day.

2

0% Feeling

*Love binds feelings on the solid rock of faith and ties
passion within the sacrificial cord of promise.*

She glowed before the crowd.

She was an eighth grader in my middle school. She was
bubbly, popular, and cute. She was a cheerleader and Diane was
her name.[1]

Three hearts were smitten by her beauty. My seventh grader
heart was among them.

Individually, none of us had the grit to approach her. Together,
we found courage and joined forces to write a poetic letter to
capture her heart. I was the scribe in the group.

The day came and we delivered the passionate letter.

Unfortunately, Diane shared the love poem with her
boyfriend. As a result, hell erupted. Like an angry lioness
protecting her cub, the boyfriend flexed his anger to chase us
away like uninvited scavengers.

Enraged with jealousy, he vented his fury on us.

Fear gripped our souls.

For a week, the boyfriend hounded us and chased our feelings for Diane to extinction.

He uttered threats and dared us with words: "I am going to beat each one of you."

For a week, we scrambled to save our lives. During recess and lunchtime, we stayed near classrooms to be within the protection of teachers.

We were grateful when the school janitor stepped in. He calmed all of us, sorted the issue, and tamed the angry boyfriend.

The janitor ordered one of us to arm-wrestle Diane's beau. Tall and packed with muscles, my friend beat the jealous boyfriend. Diane's lover was silenced and humbled. He became more willing to hear the janitor's demand.

The janitor ordered the three of us to shake hands with Diane's boyfriend and told us: "Find another girl."

Love smiled that day.

This drama with Diane was a gem. It was a priceless gift from heaven.

From this experience, I moved forward with a precious life lesson.

From this trial, my eyes opened to the reality of love.

I made a youthful vow and a promise to God that day. This pledge may have been prompted by fear, ignorance, or desperation. However, this promise became one of my guiding beacons.

As I look back, I cherish my naive pursuit of love.

This youthful drama saved me years of needless pain, pointless hurts, and painful mistakes. As a result, I did not have to carry as much excess baggage.

Bright Wrappings

Feelings stay when welcomed and fade when ignored.

They wilt when love is withheld. They get lonely when isolated and grieve when violated. Emotions can be swayed by the food you eat, the weather, and the people around.

Feelings blend with the scene like a chameleon.

They cower when exposed and hide when embarrassed. Feelings run when scared, bend when pressured, follow the latest rhythm, and change on a whim.

Feelings lure the heart to go everywhere but abandon the soul when things get rough.

You cannot trust feelings or depend on changing moods to guide your life. *"Deceit is in the heart of those who devise evil, but counselors of peace have joy"* (Prov. 12:20).

Do not allow feelings to direct your passion, your life, or your destiny. Before you conduct an emotional exchange, know the price, know the impact, and know the will of God.

Life requires choices.

Love involves a 100 percent choice. Therefore, command your feelings to step aside and move them away from the driver's seat of your life.

When you choose, you declare your essence and exercise your God-given will. When you choose, life is no longer a mishap. Love is no longer an accidental short burst of passion. Love is more than a feeling; it is a choice.

No matter how strong the resolve, feelings alter your outlook. Feelings blind your eyes, shatter your poise, and drain your energy. *"The heart is deceitful above all things, and desperately wicked; who can know it?"* (Jer. 17:9).

Feelings bait the eyes to focus on bright wrappings rather than contents. Feelings goad the heart to rush at things that bring immediate pleasure to the body and hasty resolve to the restless mind. As a result, feelings give the heart an aimless, bumpy ride. At some point, the soul slows down, stops, and rests. But the wayward heart will ride again on a roller coaster of emotions with no direction, no purpose, and no meaning.

Through time, feelings give up their glamour, but love remains true and pure.

In marriage, a man and a woman choose to love each other. As time passes, lustrous feelings may fade and lose their charm. Over time, wrinkles dig deeper on her face. Soon, hairs on his head will flee. The roughness of life causes the skin to harden and loses its glow.

Festive options tempt the heart away from solemn promises. However, the love, the bond, and the vow bring the heart home. Love binds feelings on the solid rock of faith and ties passion within the sacrificial cord of promise.

Broken hearts

The history of mankind, the story of my life, and the story of your life are summed up as a journey to find God's love.

Sadly, by choice, many will not go toward God. Many walk in gloom searching for joy, peace, meaning, and love. They nurse broken lives and look to others, who also have weighty issues to bear, for answers.

Is your journey moving you away from God?

If so, stop!

If you are stuck in emotional quicksand, stop. If you are drowning is an ocean of sin, stop. Reclaim your bearing by crying out to God. Reach out to Christ, the great Captain who rescues shipwrecked lives.

Jesus says, *"Come to Me, all you who labor and are heavy laden, and I will give you rest. Take My yoke and learn from Me, for I am gentle and lowly in heart, and you will find rest for you souls. For My yoke is easy and My burden is light"* (Matt. 11:28-30).

QUESTIONS TO SEARCH YOUR SOUL

A. What are traits of love?

   Read 1 Corinthians 13. (See Appendix II.)
   Complete the worksheet: Love Is . . . (See Appendix III.)
   Share love with people each day.

B. Daily life: *Unleash the Beauty and Power of Love* to your friends

   Create a loving place for friends.
   Find simple ways to love people.
   Each day, share tokens of love with people.

C. Self-discovery

   Read the Bible to find your purpose.
   Define the love you want to experience each day.
   Define the love you want to share with others.

3

Love Is . . .

Love is the currency of life. You share love and you receive love. The quality of life demands pureness of passion and lasting legacy depends on how you share love with others.

In the arena, emotional bombshells explode.

Feelings erupt inside yearning souls. Hearts search for relief to ease the longings inside. Wayward minds hunt for peace, shattered lives look for refuge, and broken hearts seek love. Many dwell in the teeth of hell while others abide in the arms of joy. All hope to see and feel love again.

Love lightens burdened minds, soothes parched souls, and heals violated hearts.

"Love suffers long and is kind; love does not envy; love does not parade itself, is not puffed up; does not behave rudely, does not seek its own, is not provoked, thinks no evil; does not rejoice in iniquity, but rejoices in the truth; bears all things, believes all things, hopes all things, endures all things" (1 Cor. 13:4-7).

For some, the journey of passion has not started. For others, the heart's quest has just begun. For many, the journey continues.

How about you?

How is the journey of life?

How is your journey of love?

Buried by hate but transformed by love

A pastor was arrested for his faith in Christ.[1]

Prison guards tortured him.

Soldiers took the pastor, his wife, and young children to a nearby mountain.

When they reached the site, one soldier nudged a shovel at the pastor's hands and ordered the man of God dig a hole.

Hours passed.

The pastor dug a deep pit. Then, a soldier took the shovel and commanded the preacher to get on his knees in the pit.

Seconds later, the other soldier gave the shovel to the pastor's wife and told her to scoop the dirt back in the hole.

Immediately, she balked.

However, the soldier pointed the barrel of the gun to her head. She sobbed.

With loving eyes, she looked at her husband.

Slowly, she scooped the dirt. As dirt bounced off her husband's head, tears flowed from her eyes. With each stroke, pain pierced her heart. With each scoop of earth, her soul ripped open. The children saw what was happening and tried to hold on to the shovel. However, the loving wife kept scooping the dirt back in the hole.

Her husband said, "Do not be afraid; be strong in the Lord."

As dirt piled over his shoulder, the husband said, "I love you and God loves you."

The ordeal was painful for the wife and terrifying for the children. The children screamed in terror as their father was buried alive.

Seasons passed.

Hearts changed.

During a bright, calm morning, two men knelt on the ground where the pastor was buried.

They sobbed.

Tears gushed from their eyes.

With contrite hearts, both asked forgiveness. With solemn gratitude, both thanked the pastor for his courage to love.

These men were the soldiers ordered by their leaders to bury the pastor alive. Now, they carry the message of the man of God. Now, they share the love of Christ to a hateful hurting world.

Chosen path

Love is the theme of each life drama.

Love is the currency of life. You share love and you receive love. Love etches deeper relationships. The quality of life demands pureness of passion and lasting legacy depends on how you share love with others.

You shape a life by the way you give and receive love. You define life by the way you translate love into action. Character deepens when you share love, but becomes shallow, reckless, and selfish when the heart is programmed only to receive.

Love defines you.

Hate also shapes a life.

With love, you walk with pedigreed passion. With hate, you walk with tainted desire. Love puts the heart under the spotlight of truth. But hate pulls the soul to darkened nooks of depravity.

Each day, love and hate jostle one another to control your life. Each day, love or hate etches a mark on your soul.

Darkness lures the mind from every side. And sadly, many cradle anger, nurse old wounds, and cuddle heart pains.

Millions trap their souls behind bars of hate. As a result, broken hearts clog the highway of life, waiting to be towed out of the fast lane of despair. Many travel on dark paths of loose morals and walk on crooked trails of deceit. Some wade in murky pools of hurts and slog through muddy roads of failures.

Others park their lives on roads of sadness. Their dreams flattened, their spirit discharged, and their souls battered. They exist in pain and wait to rust away their burdened lives.

While life provides wondrous vistas, it is a challenge. Many struggle with fear as they drown their souls in the past.

Youthful souls live on the edge of death while marching forward to find the gift of life. They are eager because they have not tasted the bitterness of life. Time will tell of their exploits and what they become.

On the other hand, some unveil the truth about love. They realize true love is God-given. As a result, the world shines brighter because they touch our lives.

Are you one of them?

Are you shining with love?

Many go through life without knowing the way to live, the road to joyful moments, or the love of God. Others do not find meaning and purpose, and go back to the ground with sadness in their souls.

God has placed love in the soul. Its presence is crucial. Its impact on life is vital.

The baby step to *Unleash the Beauty and Power of Love* involves looking at yourself in the mirror. See the image. Stare at the person glaring back. Ask the question, "Do I know you?"

How well do you know this person?

Is this person a stranger?

Get to know the person in the mirror. Do not let the image move out from your sight. Do not let the person wander away. Tie the person with virtue and anchor the person in truth.

Each day, take time to see yourself in the reflecting glass.

Search your soul.

See the ugliness of hate and feel the hurt of a broken life. Accept the pain of living, learn from the scars of defeats, and cherish the

H. C. Villanueva

blessings of today. At the same time, pull dreams bestowed from heaven and take simple steps toward the grace of God.

Each day, unleash the love inside. Let it fill your soul and flow from your heart.

Ignite the power granted by God. Nurture the passion to live, express love without conditions, and freely share grace from heaven. Then, go on a journey to find more of God and unfold your life by sharing your goodness, your kindness, and your love with others.

As you persevere, great things will come through. As you remain steadfast, you overcome obstacles. As you seek God, you break free from the bondage of sin. Hope prevails when you persist, and doors open when you knock with firmness.

Be like the psalmist who said, *"I waited patiently for the LORD; and He inclined to me, and heard my cry. He also brought me up out of a horrible pit, out of the miry clay, and set my feet upon a rock, and established my steps"* (Ps. 40:1, 2).

Reach out to God.

Take small steps to share love each day. Keep sharing your kindness. Keep doing godly deeds, for in due time fruits of your work will ripen.

Even within the vastness of eternity, each moment of life is meant to be special. When life comes to an end, let these be your final words, "Love is . . . Love is beautiful. Love is heavenly. I am content, fulfilled, and I have lived a meaningful life for God."

QUESTIONS TO SEARCH YOUR SOUL

A. What is love?

What is the quality of love you have been sharing?
What is the quality of your life?
Write seven ways to share love each day.

B. Daily life: *Unleash the Beauty and Power of Love* to your neighbor

A neighbor is a person with whom you come in contact
each day.
A neighbor is a friend at work, school, or in the community.
Create a loving place for your neighbors.

C. Self-discovery

Each morning, stand in front of the mirror.
Ask the question, "How can I better my life today?"
Get in touch with your inner self each day.

4

Two Voices

Pride acts gently at first. However, once it enters the soul, pride builds a towering fortress in the heart. Once engulfed in pride, only the power of God can free the soul from its grip.

Two forces present themselves each day to control your heart, your soul, and your life.

One screams to lure your attention, arrest your will, and capture your precious time. The other stands calm.

Often, you choose the louder voice.

Take time to know the subtle nuances of each voice and see the clues they leave behind. When you pause in silence, you hear their voices, feel their essence, and see their impact.

Know these forces well. These characters sway your life and influence who you are, what you become, and where you are going.

These forces are pride and love.

One is truthful; the other lies. Both influence your life.

They are gatekeepers to your emotions and key holders to your future.

For a moment, pride looks nice.

Pride allures with appeal. It glitters, entices, and smiles. Pride says soothing words to charm your heart.

You may detect its true face. Initially, pride is gentle. However, once the soul gives it access, pride builds a towering fortress in the heart. Once engulfed in pride, only the power of God can free the soul from its grip.

Pride appears agreeable from a distance. Yet, when you look closely, pride loses its allure, its appeal, and its aura. When pride bares its true face, it is ugly and gets uglier each day.

You do not have to worry about love.

Love guides the soul to the truth.

It sets life on an honest path. Love discards deceit without delay and without regret. Love reveals the truth, even though it may inflict momentary pain. In the end, love raises the soul on a pedestal and drapes the heart with joy.

Pride and love contrast one another.

Pride says, "Do not yield a magnifying glass. Do not provide truths to see you through. They will see your blemishes, faults, and shortcomings. They will not like your lack, failure, or pain. Instead, give them sunglasses. Darken their hearts, blind their souls, and confuse their minds."

Love, on the other hand, says, "Help them. Provide truth to help them see your heart more clearly."

"Be patient. Be honest. Be open."

Choices

You are dared every day and challenged at each step.

Move with courage to reach out to God. *"For the LORD God is a sun and shield; the LORD will give grace and glory; no good thing will He withhold from those who walk uprightly"* (Ps. 84:11).

When you persist, you come out ahead. When you persevere, you are strengthened. When you seek God, He will be there.

What resides in your heart?

Is it pride? Is it love?

The influence of pride is a daily reality. You cannot turn pride on today and turn it off tomorrow.

Neither love nor pride is a hitchhiker, but the face people see every day. The voice people hear. The essence people feel.

Pride and love does not ride with you for a short distance. They ride with you wherever you go.

Pride makes the heart feel good for a short time.

Pride says, "You look great. The charade must go on. The show must proceed."

Pride looks nice for a fleeting moment in the limelight.

Pride takes a lonely heart to a desolate corner. Pride works best in the dark. It parades false hope and drags the soul to despair.

When pride reigns, the soul cannot avoid life's booming fall. The soul crashes against the rock of pain. Loss of discipline lures the heart to a whirlpool of deceit.

As moments pass, life diminishes.

Deep inside, the heart feels empty. Deep down inside, the soul is lonely.

Without hope, life shrivels in darkness.

Without faith, the mind remains stagnant in the dark. Without love, the heart drowns in emptiness. However, God is near to rescue battered lives.

In the Bible, Solomon shared timeless advice:

"Remember your Creator before the silver cord is loosed,
Or the golden bowl is broken,
Or the pitcher shattered at the fountain,
Or the wheel broken at the well.
Then the dust will return to the earth as it was,
And the spirit will return to God who gave it"

(Eccles. 12:6, 7).

Truth takes over

Pride lessens the value of life.

A prideful soul is a deep abyss that cannot be filled. Wants tug the heart to endless desires. In the end, pride hardens the heart, takes the soul on a whirlwind journey, and blinds the mind to the truth.

When pride guides, life is fun, wild, and short-lived. Blemished desires perform a brief dance. Dark passion excites the heart behind closed doors. The devious mind enjoys each tainted morsel of thought. However, a sin-laden heart is never satisfied. *"For where envy and self-seeking exist, confusion and every evil thing are there"* (James 3:16).

When pride pushes the soul to the edge, the charade stops. The show stops. The spent life is cornered. Then, truth takes over. Many wonder why bad things happen. The mind searches for the culprit. However, the answer simmers inside. It is in our doing. We allow the sin of pride control the will and corrupt the mind.

If you are in this drama, stop.

Look to God.

Ask God for help.

Let God touch your soul and change your life. Let love touch your dreams, your frailties, and your past. As you share the goodness within, you lessen the influence of hate, greed, and pride. As God works in you, you weaken the grip of sin on your life.

Engage life to *Unleash the Beauty and Power of Love*.

Be a doer of what is good.

Share love with all.

QUESTIONS TO SEARCH YOUR SOUL

A. What is the voice speaking within?

> Hate or love? Pride or sacrifice? Lies or truth?
> Examine the thoughts lingering in your mind.
> Find ways to improve your thought pattern.

B. Daily life: *Unleash the Beauty and Power of Love* to the world

> Create a loving place for people around you.
> Find simple ways to love people.
> Have a plan to share love with people each day.

C. Self-discovery

> Listen to God. He is speaking.
> Today, listen for His voice: *"Do not harden your hearts . . ."*
> (Ps. 95:8a).
> Say, "Speak, Lord." Then, see tokens God places on your path.

5

Just Me, the Voice Crying Within

I

You woke up early this morning, and
I greeted you with a gentle warm, "Hello."

You were absorbed with life and you treated
me like a stranger you did not know.

You looked at the mirror, fixed your hurts,
blemishes, and failed to take a look at me.

You ventured into the world with your dreams and
failed to bring me to where you want to be.

You tried hard to go up to a high mountain
but cannot find true peace, contentment, and love.

During lonely moments, you cried out loud but
failed to look at the One who is from above.

You shared laughter with strangers; I was there
standing and you did not ask me to draw nigh.

Day by day, year by year, you walked away
from your true self as your short life passed by.

Part Two

SHARING THE HEART

Part Two: **Sharing the Heart**

CHECKLIST

Principles to instill

- A solemn beauty surrounds a saddened soul.

- Love gives you courage to face today.

- When God works through you, love gets powerful.

Things to do

- Answer the question, "What will I sacrifice for love?"

- Know the life you want to share today.

- Create a sharing place for family, friends, and neighbors.

A life to build

- Each day, share love with family, friends, and neighbors.

- Know the people around you.

- Encourage people working at stores, gas stations, etc.

6

Love Is Powerful

To share love in the arena of life, you open the vault of your heart and disburse gems polished by God.

Love is potent.

"Love never fails" (1 Cor. 13:8a). Love enriches the scene, lightens the journey, and sweetens the soul. Love is the essence all yearn to possess. Love holds life together. Also, love is like glue that binds us as one.

You sow love by giving part of your life. You impart love by sharing your time, your kindness, and your goodness.

Love has a price tag. Something has to be sacrificed. Something has to be given in order to garner its power. Something has to be given in order to feel its beauty. You "give" love away in order to garner more life.

"For whoever desires to save his life will lose it, but whoever loses his life for My sake will find it" (Matt. 16:24).

You give love in order to find more love.

To share love in the arena of life, you open the vault of your heart and disburse gems polished by God.

This is a story, a journey, of a man living without love.[1]

When he was young, the father tortured the family. With anguish, he saw his mom speared with unkind words and endured the banter and abuse of a drunkard.

The family struggled.

The parents divorced.

During the next couple of years, the young man lived with his mother. However, he clashed with her authority and ran away from home.

While homeless, alcohol drowned his soul and drugs numbed his heart.

He brought pain to himself and those around him.

As darkness shackled his soul, no one showed him how to love. No one showed him how to live. As a result, the promise of a radiant life dimmed.

As he grew older, the life of his father played out again. Like a tape recorder, he replayed scenes of his childhood. He abused his wife with sharp vicious words and hurled cruel harsh verbal jabs at his son.

Sunday came

Something happened.

God knocked at the door of his heart. It was not an accident. It was not a coincidence.

Early in the morning, a friend asked him to drink. A few cans of alcohol turned to cases. And the one-hour get-together turned into an all-day drinking marathon.

Then, it was time to go home.

He was not in the right frame mind to be with his family. He was abusive and violent.

Sunday came.

His wife gave an ultimatum. She said, "This is it. It is over. I want a divorce!"

For a moment, reality brought down the hammer of truth. The demand shook his soul. Truth exposed itself harshly. It was firm and unbending.

This time he was forced to face his reality. This time he was forced to choose.

He had two choices.

He could either live the same life or embrace a new direction. He could harden his heart or walk another path. He could live in denial or choose to live a godly life.

He chose the latter. He wanted to change. He wanted to live.

With a contrite heart, he begged his wife for another chance.

This time, he was serious.

This time, he wanted to change.

This time, he was true to his word.

He signed up for an alcoholic support group. It was a token to his wife that he was letting go of the old dark ways.

Then, his wife asked him to go to church. At first, he sneered at the notion. However, after many invitations, he agreed to go.

During a Sunday church service, tears welled up in his eyes. For an unknown reason, conviction grabbed his heart and truth exposed his darkened life.

The pastor spoke to him as if he was the only one in the audience and the message was meant for him.

This time truth was gentle. This time truth was soothing. This time truth was liberating, uplifting, and refreshing.

Realization set in and he wept.

The wayward life was stopped, the hardened soul was confronted, and the sinful heart found grace. At that moment, he made a life-changing choice.

He gave his heart to Jesus Christ. (See Appendix 1: Your Greatest Confession.)

The decision started the cleansing process. The choice allowed the change. The new resolve began the transformation.

God meets you there

The change started many years ago.

He never looked back. He is now "a new man" with a godly heart.

Now he can say, *"I press toward the goal for the prize of the upward call of God in Jesus Christ"* (Phil. 3:14).

He is happy and the family is happy.

He found a reason to live. He wakes up each morning thanking God.

Now, he can freely say, *"I have been crucified with Christ and it is no longer I who live, but Christ lives in me; and the life which now I live in the flesh, I live by faith in the Son of God, who loved me and gave himself for me"* (Gal. 2:20).

Truth becomes clearer when the soul is humble.

Change comes more quickly when the heart greets truth willingly.

Sunday draws near when you want to change.

No matter where you are, truth will meet you.

No matter where you are in life, God meets you there.

If you are lonely, God is there with you. If you are hurting, God is near to comfort you. If you are lost, God is there to show you the truth.

Change is easy.

However, we make the process of change painful, harder, and longer. We are afraid to change. We are afraid to let go. We are afraid to be exposed and we are not willing to release the control of our lives. We are afraid of the truth and hold tightly to our dark ways.

We waste precious years learning truths that were meant to free us from bondage. We walk on darkened paths and go through spin cycles of sin, void of peace, joy, and love. We falter many times before accepting that God's ways are better. Sadly, many go to the grave clinging to tainted desires--without peace, without hope, and without love.

When we fail to love, the tarnished heart prevents our eyes from seeing the beauty of life. Greed forces the soul to settle for leftover morsels. Pride entices the heart to settle for cheap passion, short-lived fun, and temporary peace. As a result, the heart wanders in the desert of sin--lonely, parched, and empty.

If you are drowning in despair or roasting in the oven of hate, stop.

Be still.

Ask God for help. He will be there when you are ready. God hears you when you cry out.

God heals battered souls with love.

Love lightens minds searching for acceptance, soothes wounded hearts crying in the darkest of night, and mends broken souls drowning in despair. God heals shattered lives and provides strength to face the challenges of today.

"Be anxious for nothing, but in everything by prayer and supplication, with thanksgiving, let your requests be made known to God; and the peace of God, which surpasses all understanding, will guard your hearts and minds through Christ Jesus" (Phil. 4:6, 7).

QUESTIONS TO SEARCH YOUR SOUL

A. What are you sharing with others?

Selfish desire? Unconditional love? Lustful wants?
Find the essence of your soul.
What blessing can you share today?

B. Daily life: *Unleash the Beauty and Power of Love* to your family

Create a sharing place for your family.
Each day, share tokens of love with family members.
A smile, a word of praise, or short notes of love are some
gifts you can share today.

C. Self-discovery

If you can change your life, what will you do?
What is the first simple step? Second step? Third step?
What can you do today?

7

Heart Check

*We satisfy sin without checking the cost. In the
process, we hurt others and ourselves.*

I met Mr. and Mrs. Moore during a Las Vegas convention.[1]

They had been married over sixty-four years. The beauty of
their lives shone. Both glowed with warm smiles. The aura on
their faces matched. Their speech pattern reflected one another.
They were like two violins playing in unison.

I asked Mr. Moore, "What is the secret to your marriage?"

He paused for a moment.

Then, Mr. Moore, with a jolly smile, said, "It's commitment."

Mr. Moore paused for another moment and churned years of
memories.

The aged skin on his forehead wrinkled as he scooped
precious memories from the bottom of his soul.

Again, with a twinkle in his eyes, he said, "Yeah, it's
commitment. You have fights. But they are part of life. However,
when you are pledged in marriage, you are glued to each other.
You live in harmony and solve challenges together."

"Two are better than one, because they have a good reward for their labor. For if they fall, one will lift up his companion" (Eccles. 4:9-10a).

Mr. Moore is remarkable. After sixty-four years of marriage, romance rumbles in his heart. He came to the convention to share love poems about his love for his wife.

Even in their twilight years, passion burns hot in their souls. Their bodies are now frail, but their love grows stronger.

Deep wrinkles etch their faces, but love glows richly from their hearts.

They are chained to one another with respect, patience, and passion. As a result, their love is lasting, their love is rich, and their love is infectious.

Sugar-coated highways

Love has no easy paths.

Love does not travel on selfish freeways or engage in one-night motel trysts. Love does not drive on sugar-coated highways of deceit or on fast lanes of shifting emotions.

Love waits on short streets of patience and travels on dusty roads of perseverance. Love travels to its destination on straight route of promises pausing at rest stops of care.

Some paths to love do not have lights. Some of life's back roads do not have signs. As a result, we need a Guide to help us navigate life's winding roads. We need a Light when life darkens. We need a Teacher to bring truth to twisted minds, and we need a Healer to mend broken lives.

As we travel, we need to listen to the voice of God. We need to hearken to the guidance and warning of God.

Sadly, many ignore the warning signals and remain in motion until hopes are dashed, dreams are shattered, and bodies are shriveled.

How about you?

Are you traveling on bustling highways of life?

Do you stop to refresh your soul?

Do you perform heart checks?

Warning systems

The body has many warning systems.

Before you sneeze, the body gives you an alarm signal.

When toxic gas or dust particles enter the nose, they pass through highly sensitized hairs. When particles touch the hairs, they create reactions. These sensations are relayed to the brain and trigger the body to sneeze.

The conscience works under the same principle. The conscience tells the heart what is right and what is wrong. However, we often ignore these warning signals.

Day-to-day choices adjust the sensitivity of the heart. Sadly, many ignore small changes until the heart hardens with pride, the soul burns with hate, and the mind simmers with devious thoughts.

The conscience reacts like lungs to smoke. When a person takes the first puff of smoke, violent coughing occurs. The lungs reject the dangerous particles entering the body.

The second puff of smoke still may cause violent coughs. After the third, fourth, or fifth time, the body adjusts.

After a while, lungs are besieged with nicotine and lose their sensitivity.

Then, cancer may set in.

The soul reacts in the same manner. When the heart is soiled with sin, the soul first reacts with intensity. Then, the heart hardens, habits cake in, and the mind twists toward deviousness.

When the heart is violated, the soul searches for answers. Instead of looking to God, many look for quick fixes.

How about you?

Do you stop to check your heart?

Do you stop to check your soul?

Reflection

Sunday is a great time to pause to check the progress of life and the condition of the heart.

The specific day is not important. However, what is important is setting aside time to pray, to dream, and to plan.

Spend a full day each week in rest and reflection. Get to know who you are, where you are going, and what you are becoming. During your day of rest, ask God to help you calm your mind, rest your body, and relax your heart.

Say, *"Search me, O God, and know my heart; try me, and know my anxieties; and see if there is any wicked way in me, and lead me in the way everlasting"* (Ps. 139:23, 24).

One Sunday afternoon, I reflected on an incident from past homeless outreach. We had given clothes and household items to those in need. I monitored a table offering cups, pans, glassware, and toys.

A little girl chose four toys. She cuddled them with her arms. I offered a small plastic bag for her to secure her prized possessions.

She accepted.

The bag began to be stuffed so I offered a cardboard box. She accepted and transferred the toys. With excitement, she continued picking more toys.

When other kids picked toys from her box, I moved the box closer to her. The little girl was protective of her toys.

The children helped me see the simple things of life. The young ones stopped me for a moment. The little ones helped me search my soul and pulled tears from my heart.

As adults, we look for things to fill our lives. They may be careers, possessions or kinships. We collect toys to fill the emptiness. We hoard things to soothe our longing hearts. We keep on grabbing until we are stuffed. We satisfy sin without checking the cost. In the process, we hurt others and ourselves.

H. C. Villanueva

Another incident touched my heart.

A father rode a bike to an unpaved parking lot. The young son sat on a cart attached to the bike. The boy looked hungry and sat silently.

Volunteers went to action. The people at the gifting table gave the family clothes and a blanket. Volunteers at the food table offered a plate of food and a cherry pie.

For a moment, the boy's stomach was filled.

The food gave him strength to face another day. The blanket gave him warmth for the night. However, looking back, we missed what he needed most. This simple thing costs nothing. However, it required caring hearts to open and time to be spent.

Children need love and guidance. *"Train up a child in the way he should go, and when he is old he will not depart from it"* (Prov. 22:6).

At an early age, young ones need support. We need to etch hope on their lives and soak them with love to give them courage to face today. We need to mold their character, nurse their dreams, and guide their minds to the truth. Also, we need to lead their souls toward God.

Giving them love tells them they matter. Love gives their souls strength to help them conquer the trying moments of today.

We, too, need people to tell us that we are loved. This gesture of compassion gives us courage to face life. By the same token, love helps us take one more step forward.

As adults, we need love, too. We soothe our souls with things. We adorn our lives with bright wrappings. Fame, riches, power, wealth, and shiny toys garnish our lives. We falsely declare that we are happy. But deep down inside, we are neither happy nor content. Deep down inside, we are lonely and want to cry out for help.

QUESTIONS TO SEARCH YOUR SOUL

A. Do you perform heart checks?

Spend four hours each week thinking about your life, dreams, and faith in God.

Know your God-given skills.

Spend time finding ways to improve your life.

B. Daily life: *Unleash the Beauty and Power of Love* to your friends

Create a sharing place with friends.

When a friend shares a noble idea or dream, say, "Tell me more. Give me more details."

Then say, "What are you going about it today? What is the first step?"

C. Self-discovery

Paint love in your heart before you get out of the door each morning.

What will happen to you if you do this?

What will happen to people around you when you paint love in their hearts?

8

Souls in the Desert

You cannot close your heart, ignore the hurting world around you, and be content with life.

One Monday morning, I came an hour early.

At 8:05 am, I was to meet my Bible study group.

A man sat three tables away from where I waited. At first, I did not pay attention to his presence.

Seconds later, smoke filled the small courtyard.

Then, the man's uninvited cough stirred the stillness of the quiet morning.

I listened to the violent coughing and glanced at the man. He was the homeless person living around the shopping center. His clothes were torn; dirt and body oil caked on his white shirt; and large sores wrapped around his ankles.

As the smoke got thicker, the coughs turned more stubborn.

I yelled in my mind, "Sir, throw the cigarette away! It will stop your coughing."

I did not speak, but concern for the man raced through my mind.

The man stood and continued to enjoy puffs of smoke between coughs. The violent hacking stayed with him as he moved away from the scene.

How about you?

It may not be from cigarettes, drugs, or alcohol. It may not be anger, hate, or pride. Whatever it may be, you cough life issues. You lose focus, get distracted, and ignore miracles brewing inside.

Many plead with you to stop. However, you close your heart from seeing the truth and lock life in bondage.

You cannot close your heart, ignore the hurting world around you, and be content with life.

You have a choice.

You can fade from the scene, go deeper into darkness, and sink lower into despair . . . or go toward God and walk in His love.

Be like David, who prayed, *"As the deer pants for the water brooks, so pants my soul for You, O God. My soul thirst for God, for the living God. When shall I come and appear before God?"* (Ps. 42:1, 2).

Hoarding

Society keeps moving faster and faster into oblivion.

Technology allows us to do things quickly. Cars and planes move us swiftly. Cell phones and the Internet quicken dialogues. We should have more time for family, dreams, and aspirations. Also, we should have more time to pause and look, stop and consider, plan and work.

We neglect precious time. We narrow our vision, lower our outlook, and shorten our reach.

We become selfish. We live in haste and get hasty results. We hurry life and have shallow relationships. We yearn for a better life, but may not be willing to change.

How soon do you want to change?

A split second? Eleven days? Forty years?

Never?

Moses led the people out of bondage (Exodus 1-40).

Then, the Promised Land was nearby. However, the people hardened their hearts and grumbled when there was no water.

When food rained from heaven, they hoarded. People rebelled and complained. As a result, they traveled in the desert for forty years.

Freed from bondage, the Israelites latched onto the past. The older generation looked back and wanted the comfort of slavery.

The blessing was a short distance away. However, they missed the peace, the joy, and the life offered to them.

All they had to do was obey. But, they did not open their hearts to God. As a result, God did not allow the older generation to enter the land of promise.

How about you?

Are you living in the desert of life?

If so, how long are you going to be parched under the hot sun?

Eleven days? Forty years?

Always?

You decide how long you stay in the desert of sin.

You choose how long you stay in strife.

Are you lost?

A father drives around the block.

The son asks, "Are we lost?"

The father says, "No, we are not. We are making good progress."

They go through the streets a couple more times.

The son asks again, "Are we lost?"

"No, I know where we are going," says the proud father.

They go around the block one more time.

Life is like that.

Pride prevents eager souls from reaching their destination sooner. Many toil in folly, swim in foibles, and waddle in hurts. They go through life without asking for help. Some walk in dark alleys of life and go around the block many times. Others travel on wrong paths and waste a lifetime.

How about you?

Do you go deeper into gloom?

Do you go around the block over and over again?

When life is tangled, move closer to God. God uncurls twisted pasts and transforms rumpled lives. God calms hearts during violent ordeals and guides souls through vague moments.

What do you do when life falls apart?

Stop. Pause. Be still.

Ask God for help. Seek His guidance to help you move out of the desert of life. The Bible says, *"But those who wait on the LORD shall renew their strength; they shall mount up with wings like eagles, they shall run and not be weary, they shall walk and not faint"* (Isa. 40:31).

QUESTIONS TO SEARCH YOUR SOUL

A. What do you do when life falls apart?

   Do you have a pre-plan to solve life issues?
   Do you stop and consider the journey at hand?
   Write solutions for issues like rejection, failure, and pain ...
   before they occur again.

B. Daily life: *Unleash the Beauty and Power of Love* to your neighbors

   Create a sharing place for neighbors.
   Get to know them.
   Find common interests.

C. Self-discovery

   Listen to your inner voice.
   Monitor what you are saying to yourself.
   Stop parroting problems. Start sharing solutions.

9

Wrapped in Pain

Do not waste your energy pursuing imagined problems.
Focus on blaring issues you can face today.

I sat on a bench under an old monkey pod tree.

Then, a ball of bees fell and flopped inches from my shoes. At first, I was not alarmed and paid little attention. Seconds later, the world around me buzzed. They were angry. Bees swarmed with vengeance as if they had issues to settle.

I tried to chase them away with my bare hands. That did not work. I swatted the bees with sheets of paper. That did not work either.

I whacked the bees a couple more times. To no avail. Bees kept swarming around me with a fury.

I walked twenty feet away from the tree but the pesky bees still buzzed nearby. However, fewer bees tried to get a piece of me. I swatted the bees a couple of times. Again, to no avail. The effort did not work.

I moved another twenty feet away from the tree. The vengeance faded, and the bees began to fly away and leave me alone.

The frantic seconds felt like an eternity.

After the ordeal, I paused for a moment.

A throbbing pain pulsed above my eye. I raced an index finger across my forehead and felt a lump. I was stung.

I did not get mad at the pesky bees. It would be useless and would not solve the problem.

Instead, I relaxed my mind, took slow deep breaths, and thanked God only one bee injected its poison.

I stopped for a moment and lay on the grass of the grounds of Iolani Palace.[1]

My eyes scanned the sky and gazed at the late afternoon sun. The calm blue sky soothed my soul. Cool, gentle wind rustled the leaves and cooled my body.

I relaxed my heart, calmed my soul, and slowed down my breathing.

I realized I was resting on grassy piece of paradise and recognized that people around the world go through much worse situations.

They feel the sting of life. They face the sting of pain, carry the sting of grief, and endure the sting of emptiness.

After a soul-searching moment, I discerned that my condition was not that bad. As a result, I soaked the peace of the quiet afternoon.

At the end of the day, I was grateful for the bee sting. The pause allowed me to cherish what I had.

Also, I learned a priceless truth that day: When bees surround you, run away from them. Do not reason or analyze-- flee from the scene.

Stinging bees

Each day we see behavior reminiscent of angry bees.

Many bees use their stinger once and die. On the other hand, some bees use their stingers again and again.

Many bees live senseless lives and inject poison into anyone who comes near them. Some bees insert venom on purpose. This vile act is inevitable. It is their nature.

These bees I am talking about are people. They, too, are equipped with sharp stingers. They, too, inject poison into the soul.

Their stings come in many forms. It may be a fiery dart of unkind words. The stingers may be harsh comments laced with toxic words. It may be a spear of backbiting or gutter verbiage thrust in the back.

Their stingers pierce the heart and verbal toxins enter the soul. The poison dulls dreams, blunts potentials, and numbs inspirations.

What do you do when unkind words, harsh comments, and sharp backbiting words are thrown at you?

Stop.

Pause.

Be still and relax.

See the layout of the situation.

Know the nature of people. Many live with mindless dark habits while others live in pain.

You cannot blame them. They are influenced by higher powers, realms, or dark forces, and exist like zombies hurting people as they go.

"For we do not wrestle against flesh and blood, but against principalities, against powers, against rulers of the darkness of this age, against spiritual hosts of wickedness in the heavenly places" (Eph. 6:12).

People will toss their toxins at you.

Many times, it is an accident and they do not mean it. Most bees forget the incident, move on, and go to their next victim. However, you are left with the toxin, the pain, and the sting of life.

What can you change?

Do not allow harsh criticisms, unkind words, or gossips to flow in your heart.

Do not let the poison gain strength by simmering the venom in your soul.

Draw out the poison.

Forgive people who inject harsh criticisms or throw unkind words at you. *"If you forgive the sins of any, they are forgiven them; if you retain the sins of any, they are retained"* (John 20:23).

Toxins taint the purity of love, blur the clarity of the mind, and drain the joy of life. Ask God to help you flush out the toxins by forgiving those who hurt you.

You cannot control people. However, you can control your thoughts, your ideas, and your actions.

Forgive.

Most of all, love.

Do not waste your energy thinking you can change people; only God can. Do not waste your energy pursuing imagined problems. It is a useless effort.

Focus on blaring issues you can change today. Face the challenge of the moment and commit these people to God. Say, *"Teach me to do your will, for You are my God; Your spirit is good. Lead me in the land of uprightness. Revive me, O LORD, for your name's sake! For Your righteousness' sake bring my soul out of trouble"* (Ps. 143:10, 11).

A solemn beauty surrounds saddened souls. Gems of life, covered with pain, grow from battered hearts.

When life spins out of control, stop the madness. Stop the restlessness.

If you live from one jolt of reality to another or from one sting to another, take a time out, rest your mind, and refresh your soul.

Let God heal you.

QUESTIONS TO SEARCH YOUR SOUL

A. How do you handle unkind words, criticisms, and gossip?

  Have a plan to neutralize life's toxins before they are
  tossed at you.
  How do you handle unkind words?
  How do you handle criticisms?

B. Daily life: *Unleash the Beauty and Power of Love* to your world

  Create a sharing place for others.
  Praise those people serving at stores, gas stations, etc.
  Share uplifting life stories.

C. Self-discovery

  Each day, be thankful for the little things.
  Be pleased with the day you are given.
  Be grateful for the breath of air today.

10

And Ah, Spring!

Flowers bloom. Flowers fade. And Ah, spring.
The grandeur of life comes alive with the joy it brings.

I cast my solitary heart into the bright morning sun.
Not knowing what comes, what may, when all is done.

A tender blade of grass shows its promise to the world.
The newness of life, the tenderness, the covenants unfold.

A pure woman's heart is deep and vast as the mighty ocean.
Yet, my beloved sends a gentle wind to press my sail on.

Birds fly south annually. Their inner compass brings.
They come back to their roots and nurse their yearlings.

My dearest yearns a lover who is caring and God-fearing.
I am a child of heaven and know the Almighty is loving.

Spring comes. Spring goes. The rhythm of life goes on.
The beauty, the essence, the fragrance emanates around.

The promise to my love is faithfulness and commitment.
Every moment and every opportunity will be endearment.

Be ready. The beauty and splendors of life are coming soon.
And Ah Spring, be watchful. The flowers and love will bloom.

Part Three

FACETS OF LIFE

CHECKLIST

Principles to instill

- Each day comes as a gift with promise. Open the gift of life today.
- Face today. Let tomorrow take care of itself.
- You choose how you view each moment.

Things to do

- Find three time wasters. Find ways to eliminate them.
- List your challenges. Find solutions.
- Create a caring place for family, friends, and neighbors.

A life to build

- Take time to enjoy the sunsets.
- Make a habit of praising people each day.
- Be curious like a little child. Let things around you become vibrant.

11

Ashes of Yesterday

Regret robs your life. It is a thief you allow to rummage your soul and steal the precious you have been given.

To many, life plays like a broken record.

Some never skip a beat singing sad songs. They hum sad events, sad stories, and sad excuses. They never wear out repeating past mistakes, past hurts, or past pains. They sing old music with "poor me" and "blame you" melodies.

Some blame the situation, other people, the past, or even the weather to avoid taking responsibility for their lives. It is a vicious cycle of singing sad tunes.

"As a dog returns to his own vomit, so a fool repeats his folly" (Prov. 26:11).

The vomit of life feeds the mind with more foolishness, fuels the heart with more pain, and pulls the soul deeper into despair.

When living under the shadows of yesterday singing sad songs, hurts never heal, past pains never subside, and defeats continually drag souls to pools of regret. As a result, sad souls live in days gone by, ignore the present, and relive the past again and again.

I know someone who lived like a broken record player. He repeated same sad stories of failures, hurts, and disappointments.

He went through life storms. Diabetes and high blood pressure controlled his life.

One day I asked him, "How is life?"

He turned on his record player and hummed gloomy recollections of pain, hurt, and failure going back five, ten, and twenty years. After ten minutes, I knew his old sad melodies as well as the newer versions.

One day, I got wiser. I "unplugged" the record player.

When I talked to him, I did not ask, "How is life?" or "How are you?"

Instead, I guided our talks with positive ideas.

I said, "It's a great day, isn't it? The weather is beautiful. It is a blessing to be alive."

Many times, he still sang his sad melodies. However, I stopped the record player from spinning a full turn by saying, "What are you doing about it? What are your solutions?"

It took time for him to see the brighter side of life. It took time for him to change. He struggled to hum uplifting tunes. After a while, he grasped the value of singing cheerful melodies. After much effort, he now sings songs of joy, hope, and enthusiasm.

Melody of the soul

Are you singing the melody of past hurt, past opportunity, or past pain?

If you live like a broken record repeating issues of days gone by, stop.

If you are singing sad songs about yesterday, stop. If you are humming past failures, past hurts, or past problems, stop.

There are no benefits to singing sad tunes or throwing yesterday's ashes on yourself or other people.

You gain nothing good by reliving past problems, past hurts, or past issues over and over.

Instead, break the bad recordings of life by sifting lessons from failures. See hope rising from the heap of ashes. Then, compose new songs of praise and move on.

Each day, confess your dreams. Believe that brighter days come closer and situations get better.

Be grateful for what you have today. Even the small things, be grateful. Even for the obvious--the sunrise, the sunset, the breath given--be thankful.

Do not allow the tune of what you cannot do to dictate your thoughts.

Do not say your problems, your failures, or your past pains over and over. Instead, make known what God can do in you and proclaim what God can do through you.

Negative talk does not solve life issues; it adds more problems. Focusing on past problems puts an anchor to life. When problems are the lyrics of life, you are cornered, you are restless, and you will get sick.

In moments of hardship, rejection, or persecution, be like the apostle Paul who said, *"Not that I have already attained, or am already perfected; but I press on, that I may lay hold of that for which Christ Jesus has also laid hold of me. Brethren, I do not count myself to have apprehended; but one thing I do, forgetting those things which are behind and reaching forward to those things which are ahead. I press toward the goal for the prize of the upward call of God in Christ Jesus"* (Phil. 3:12-14).

Move toward God. Move forward to find the gift of life.

Pause to see gifts within. Pause to see God working in you and in the background. Dreams are placed in your soul. Destiny dances on the palms of your hands. Be aware of what you are becoming. Be aware of what you are doing with the life you have been given.

Through trials, you bake in the oven of life, and you have a choice how you come out from heated moments.

You have a choice how you unfold your life.

Regret is a thief

Life is like driving a car.

Two side mirrors called memories help you see the past. You are given an inside rear view mirror called reflection. When used properly, you move forward with confidence.

If you are driving and focused on what is behind, you hit people and things on your path and do not travel far.

By the same token, you lose view of your life when reliving the past. You lose hope when your mind is stuck on past problems, past issues, and past hurts; and you miss the chance to embrace the fullness of the moment.

Regret robs your life. It is a thief you allow to rummage your soul and steal the precious life you have been given. Regret makes you look at past failure and failed opportunities.

Thoughts of mistakes torture the mind. Regret bleeds the energy within. As a result, the present is neglected and life wastes away into hopelessness.

If you do not see lessons glowing behind you, do not look back. Keep moving forward. Do not dwell in bygone days. Do not relive past failures or past pains over and over, hoping the past will change for the better. The past will not change. It is etched in eternity.

Leave the past alone. Do not wallow in it.

Learn the lessons from the past and move on.

Sadly, many waste precious time nursing past wounds, cuddling past hurts, and stuffing their thoughts with past problems. As a result, they do not have time to live today. They do not see beautiful rainbows forming during the rain. They do not see a burdened soul refined in the furnace of adversity or see priceless pearls of joy forming in oysters of pain.

As you look back, regret fills the air.

Eternity comes closer and there is no turning back. With a few more breaths, death moves closer.

When life expires, it is over.

When death comes, you will not be able to correct past mistakes, make apologies, or have another chance at life.

In the end, you have regrets, ashes of the past, and restlessness.

Harvest life

Seeds of life are buried in yesterday. These kernels of hope are ready to sprout today.

As you nurture the seed of hope, dreams, and plans, actions bear fruit.

The long days of summer grow the fruit to maturity. But how refreshing it is when the fruits of autumn bring forth sweetness and delight.

Harvest the fruit of each moment.

Train your mind to see good in every situation--even the bad moments.

Growth depends on how many lessons you garner from each life event and freedom depends on how you sever the tentacles of former pains, and future anxieties.

Freedom is living in the present, praising God and being grateful for the life, opportunity, and hope given today.

When you look carefully and look to God, gems of life appear. *"For godly sorrow produces repentance leading to salvation, not to be regretted; but the sorrow of the world produces death"* (2 Cor. 7:10).

A diamond starts as a lifeless coal.

Intense pressure and heat change the coal into a raw, hard rock. Thereafter, a master craftsman cuts and polishes the rock into a bright gem.

By the same token, intense pressure and heated moments harden the soul. The toughness of life brings out the best or the worst in the heart. No matter how you emerge from heated moments, let the Master Craftsman cut and polish the facets of your life and let the toughness of your experience refine the soul.

First, give your life to Christ. *"Looking unto Jesus, the author and finisher of our faith, who for the joy that was set before Him endured the cross, despising the shame, and has sat down at the right hand of the throne of God"* (Heb. 12:2).

Say, "God, I have journeyed far. I give my pains, past, and sins to You. I give my dreams, aspirations, and hopes to You. Forgive me for my sins and from moving away from You. Help me. Come into my life. In Jesus' name. Amen."

Chapter 11: **Ashes of Yesterday**

QUESTIONS TO SEARCH YOUR SOUL

A. What painful events burden your life?

Are you healed from them?
What are your solutions?
What steps are you taking?

B. Daily life: *Unleash the Beauty and Power of Love* to your family

Create a caring place for family members.
Challenge them to excellence.
Give praise to each member of your family.

C. Self-discovery

If someone shares a problem with you, ask, "What are you doing about it?"
By the same token, if you are talking about your problem, stop.
Say to yourself, "What am I doing about it? What are my solutions?"

12

Challenges of Today

Nature prepares moments for the heart to feel the serenity of creation. Solemn scenes take the soul to a corner of quiet solitude. It is up to you to find peace in the midst of confusion, love in the midst of hate, and joy in the midst of pain.

"**F**or we know that the whole creation groans and labors with birth pangs together until now" (Rom. 8:22).

Each day, the sun rises and creation comes out from sacred repose.

Then, at the end of the day, nature shares glorious parting gestures. The sun gives a goodbye kiss that only nature can share. A curtain of colors covers the western sky. A red-orange ball of fire slips down the horizon. The day comes to an end. Far and near, nature smiles with gentleness.

For a moment, life slows down as the sun takes a bow. Nature allows the heart to feel the serenity of creation. Solemn scenes take the soul to a corner of quiet solitude.

For a moment, we pause. We feel our frailties, sense our hopes, and renew our dreams. Sadly, we stay in this state of awareness for only a short moment. Then, we move back to the restlessness of life.

Life unfolds at each moment and opportunities befriend willing hearts.

It is up to you to find peace in the midst of confusion, love in the midst of hate, and joy in the midst of pain.

Each new day comes with promises. Each new day brings new drama.

Each day, the stage is prepared. The props are in place. The supporting cast arrives. The audience waits and the curtain opens.

What will they see?

What will they enjoy?

What will they love?

This unfolding event is your act. This unfolding display is your life. Do not miss the show. Do not miss the drama. Be in it. Be part of the life given.

You are given time to live in fullness, not analyze its lack.

You are given passion to bestow love, not hoard its richness.

You are given chances to share your goodness, not trample on hurting souls.

You are given life to show its splendor, not throw away precious blessings.

You are given love to share its beauty, not burden society with hate.

You possess the power to show love and have a chance to share your bounties.

Each day let this be your request: *"One thing I have desired of the LORD, that I will seek: that I may dwell in the house of the LORD all the days of my life, to behold the beauty of the LORD, to inquire in His temple"* (Ps. 27:4).

As the sun sets, the day takes a bow.

Likewise, when life nears its end, life takes a bow. The drama ends and the curtain closes.

The physical body stops functioning. The body succumbs to death and becomes a lifeless shell. Yet, this is not the end. For a season, the life essence continues as a memory in people's hearts. The body goes to the ground, but the spirit lingers on to eternity.

What will they see of your life?

Will your drama be senseless?

Or will your life be a gift to people graced by your presence?

Each day comes as a bouquet of promise. Each life comes as a bouquet of potential. It is fresh with aura and crisp with hope.

God moves creation before you.

God also moves people, events, and angels so He can fulfill His promises through you. However, it is up to you to allow the fullness of heaven to show from your life.

Your spirit senses what the physical eye cannot see.

The mind sees optimism, the soul senses hope, and the heart feels love. It is up to you to find peace in the midst of confusion, love in the midst of hate, and joy in the midst of pain.

When the sun comes on the scene, many are sleeping. The new day is received by only a few.

By the same token, there are no fanfares when dreams are born and no welcoming groups when ideas give birth to new ventures.

When plans unfold, there are no bands playing.

When ideas are put to action, there are no ceremonies. Yet, dreams come with promises and hope. Sadly, few greet the promises of God.

Earthshaking events

The loss was earthshaking.

The defeat was an omen of things to come. The University of Hawaii's women's (Wahine) volleyball team went down in a heartbreaking loss after 114 consecutive conference victories. The defeat came after twelve days, a ten thousand-mile journey, and a seven-game volleyball marathon.

After the first six opponents, UH was undefeated. However, the seventh team was stalwart. Victory knocked at the door. But the long road trip drained the game intensity of the players.

The UH volleyball team won two matches to the opponent's one. They led 20-13 in the fourth set. With 10 more points, UH would win.

The eleventh-ranked Wahine went down in a hard-fought game. They lost in five sets.

The faithful fans felt the lose in stillness of the Saturday night.

Dark clouds covered the sky as Sunday morning arrived. The morning looked gloomy as gentle rain fell from heaven. Still, earthshaking events were about to unfold.

At 7:08 am, the earth shook.

The epicenter was located over one hundred sixty miles (255 km) southeast from Honolulu or ten miles (20 km) from Kailua Kona, a city on the northeast side of the island of Hawaii, Hawaii. The earthquake measured at a magnitude of 6.6.

The morning quake came as a surprise to faithful souls in the auditorium.

Lights flickered.

The floor shook.

Seconds later, everything went back to normal. However, curious minds searched for answers.

As aftershocks followed, smaller quakes triggered the automatic shut-off switch at the power sub-station.

Seconds later, the lights went out.

Darkness came in the auditorium.

Worse still, heavy rain dropped and darkened the mood of the new day. Yet, the faithful remained steadfast and calm during the morning worship.

Are you ready?

The Sunday events--earthquakes, blackout, and rain--triggered earthshaking human dramas.

A man woke up before 7:00 am. Then, the earth shook and terror filled his heart. However, he sensed the presence of God.

To this man, the message was clear. He had to live closer to God.

For this man, Sunday came and a defining moment arrived. So, he went to church.

In a dimly lit sanctuary, souls huddled near the stage. The faithful and this man received the message.

The message was, "Are you ready for the big trip? Are you ready to meet God?"

I, too, asked these questions and had soul-searching moments. Now, the spotlight turns to you *"And as it is appointed for men to die once, but after this the judgment"* (Heb. 9:27).

Are you ready for the big trip?

Are you ready to meet God?

Kindness felt

Kindness shined during the day.

A "Good Samaritan" shared power from a generator with a neighbor.

People came out of the seclusion of their homes. Hearts ventured out of emotional confines of loneliness. Lives opened as kindred souls showed kindness.

During the day, people's goodness shone through. Many extended helping hands. Love was shared among strangers. Others paused to listen to each other's souls. Many paused to feel the frailties of life.

Do we need tragic events to help us cherish what we have?

Do we need an earthquake to make us pause?

Do we need a power outage to expose our goodness?

Dark clouds, earthquakes, and huge waves will come. They are inevitable. Be prepared, for they will arrive unannounced.

By the same token, disasters in life are inevitable. They are part of life. They, too, will come unannounced. However, the misfortune should not be the focal point of a calamity. Whatever happens in life, we have to look inside and go to God. Adversities can ignite noble passions. Calamities can unlock closed minds and hardships can unleash potentials.

Let us share our goodness today.

Let us be thankful for each breath.

Let us be grateful for each blessing.

Chapter 12: **Challenges of Today**

QUESTIONS TO SEARCH YOUR SOUL

A. What are your challenges?

Write them down.
What are you going to do about them today?
What is your first simple step?

B. Daily life: *Unleash the Beauty and Power of Love* to your friends

Create a caring place for friends.
Challenge yourself and friends to do noble deeds each week.
Pray for your friends.

C. Self-discovery

Today is all you have.
What are you doing to impact others?
What are you doing today to impact eternity?

13

Tomorrow's Promises

We mortgage our future. We debit our lives to pay for short-lived fame, brief pleasure, and fleeting glitter.

"T*herefore do not worry about tomorrow, for tomorrow will worry about its own things. Sufficient for the day is its own trouble*" (Matt. 6:34).

Tomorrow flashes its promise.

Tomorrow allures with charm. Today, tomorrow stirs the mind with restlessness. Hope for tomorrow burns hot in the soul.

Thought of the next day glows like amber within. It is consuming. It will not die down and we cannot ignore it. We drop today to see what falls tomorrow.

Each new day comes with new vistas. Each new moment offers fresh bidding. We delight at the rising sun. Later on, we look for shadows to shield us from the piercing rays.

By the same token, many hide under shadows of excuse to avoid heated duties of the moment.

Others use the crutch of thinking about tomorrow to avoid the realities of today.

Wandering souls say, "Tomorrow is coming. Let us set aside the issues of today for tomorrow."

We mortgage our future.

We debit our lives to pay for short-lived fame, exploitive power, brief pleasure, and fleeting glitter.

Then, the spirit within asks, "Does living for these things fill my life? Is there more to life?"

Pride carves desires to no end. The selfish life is lifted up, lavished with shiny things, and adorned with praises.

Greed extends hands outward for more treasures, casts desires for more glitters, and grows towering egos without limits.

When the soul is lavished, the heart plans for tomorrow and looks for bigger rooms to store more desires, more wants, and more morsels. Sadly, there is no peace to a greedy heart, and there is no calm for a prideful mind. And there is no life to a sinful soul; only death.

The greedy soul does not know how to stop these longings and the greedy heart keeps on filling the vat of desires. There is no end to selfish wants.

There is no end to this madness.

At an appointed time

A sunset is a beautiful closing to the day.

Under a sunless sky, we feel tender moments. We gaze at the stars to find bearing, hug hope to comfort the heart, and look for a brighter tomorrow to soothe a doleful soul.

Day after day, we cast dreams on nets of wishes. We tangle the heart with the tentacles of tomorrow and lock the mind in the past with hurts, failures, and regrets. We drown the heart with more wants and allow the soul to wander in darkened abyss.

It costs little to relish a hopeful tomorrow. However, there is a greater price we pay.

We turn away from the chances of today.

We miss today's gift when we chase the bright lights of tomorrow.

Night after night, we try to rest our soul. We toss and turn to find peace, and we struggle to find bearing.

In the morning, the body is stressed, the mind is drained, and the soul is burdened to meet the new day. As a result, life faces the day without peace.

Today's challenges prove heavy. At the same time, tomorrow's worries are just as burdensome.

How should tomorrow be viewed?

With hope!

How should today be spent?

With love.

Love is the key to open today.

Love is the medium of exchange. You give love and receive love. Loves inspires drifting minds, directs hearts to action, and helps longing souls who have lost their way.

Engage the heart with the work at hand, because spring arrives at an appointed time and the love planted bears its fruit in due season.

They played hard

Early in the fourth quarter of the football game, the University of Hawaii Warriors scored on a three-play fifty-yard aerial blitz to the end zone.

On this night, the Hawaii signal caller completed 36 out of 47, for 419 passing yards.

There was no *aloha*[1] on the playing field for the bowl-bound University of Nevada Wolfpack. The score showed UH with 41 to Nevada's 21.

Victory was ready to open its door. The victor's crown was prepared for the Warriors.

The Warriors played hard and the mood on the sideline remained jubilant. You cannot blame them. Yet, there was so much game to be played.

The game was well in hand for the Warriors, also bowl-bound. However, during the next possession, Nevada marched to the end zone with poise.

The score read Hawaii 41, Nevada 28.

Then, with 5:32 left in the game, my friend said, "Let's leave the stadium now to avoid the traffic."

I said in a joyful mood, "Let us stay to the end and enjoy the victory."

We stayed.

Nevada played with urgency. The Wolfpack moved the ball toward the end zone. With 3:57 left, the Wolfpack scored again.

The score was now Hawaii 41 to Nevada 34.

The mood on both sides changed.

With less than three minutes, the Warriors had the ball on their own seven-yard line.

The quarterback snapped the ball and the receivers and running backs were covered. As a result, the UH quarterback scrambled to move the ball forward. In doing so, a Nevada defensive player jarred the ball and caused a fumble. Nevada claimed the ball on UH three.

With three yards to go, Nevada could tie with a touchdown and a field goal. However, the UH defense held their ground. Hawaii stopped the Wolfpack on four plays--three incomplete passes and a run for no gain.

The game was exciting.

This time, the Warriors won.

Show up

Tomorrow offers no substance for the moment. It is a distraction. It uproots your resolve and steals your time to shine today.

The fullness of today will keep you busy. Let tomorrow take care of itself. When you live today to the utmost, you do not have time to wish for tomorrow.

To win the race of life, show up.

You may not win every challenge. Still, you are a winner.

In sports, winning and losing is based on the scope of the score. However, in life, the way you prepare and the way you live offer the best trophy you can garner.

Be like the apostle Paul who said, *"But none of these move me; nor do I count my life dear to myself, so that I may finish my race with joy, and the ministry which I received from the Lord Jesus, to testify to the gospel of the grace of God"* (Acts 20:24).

As you step in the arena, you are given a chance to shine. Let your character glow. Let your life shout with compassion and let your goodness speak out loud.

In the arena of life, love is a priceless trophy, joy is a much-admired award, and peace is a much-coveted banner the heart needs.

QUESTIONS TO SEARCH YOUR SOUL

A. How do you view tomorrow?

> Write your outlook.
> Be specific.
> If tomorrow never comes, what would you do today?

B. Daily life: *Unleash the Beauty and Power of Love* to your neighbors

> Create a caring place for neighbors.
> Encourage your neighbors.
> Pray for your neighbors' well-being.

C. Self-discovery

> What is the promise of today?
> Take it. Live it. Share it.
> Be grateful for today's little things.

14

Lessons From a Little Boy

Do not go after trophies, applause, or recognition.
Live to make someone smile. Do simple things to
love yourself, others, and most of all God.

During birthdays, Christmas, and other special occasions, gifts are given.

Gifts are chosen to garnish life. At the same time, a gift is intended to make life easier. If the giver knows you, the gift is chosen to fit your life.

The gift is wrapped with shiny paper and tied with a bright ribbon. A fancy bow completes the presentation. With a joyful heart, you tear the wrapping and open the box.

You express gratitude, hold the gift with your hands, and make the gift part of your life.

However, there are darker sides to gift receiving. Many gifts are unopened. Other gifts are placed on the shelf to collect dust. Some gifts are returned, exchanged, or thrown in the garbage can.

By the same token, you are given the gift of life.

The gift is wrapped in earthen vessels. This gift is packaged in the plain wrapping of humanity. It is modest, but filled with potentials.

You have a choice.

You can take this gift or reject it.

This gift is eternal and wrapped in dust, blood, and spirit. It is bare and unassuming. Yet, the life given is dressed with love, packed with potential, and wrapped with hope.

You are a gift to yourself, to others, and to God; you have a choice to unveil your gift.

As you share your life, joy enlarges your heart and helps your soul sing with gladness in the good times and the bad. When you share the beauty within, you feel joy, contentment, and love.

People crave for love and thirst for hope.

Many live in despair and walk lonely journeys. So, let your smile warm their hearts, kind words soothe their souls, and goodness touch their lives.

Let people know they are precious and matter to God.

Hear their dreams, listen to their stories, and help them walk toward hopeful journeys.

Just be there. It means a lot to them.

When you spend time with people, you too will be encouraged.

Glimpses of heaven are in their smiles. The essence of God glows on their faces when joy bursts from their grateful soul.

No cars

It was a glorious October morning.

White puffy clouds were scattered across the sky. Cool, gentle wind from the mountain blew across the leeward side of the island of Oahu.

At 8:45 am, a little boy entered the mortgage office.

Other boys picked on him. He brought a small knife to school to protect himself. As a result, he was barred from school for one week so the mother brought him to work.

I planned to go to the bank. It was a cool day and I decided to walk on the bike path near the water of Pearl Harbor.

I asked the mother if her son could come. She agreed.

The boy liked the idea and was happy to get out of the office. He ran fifty yards ahead and slowed down. When I came closer, he ran ahead again.

We reached a stoplight and the boy wanted to cross the street. The crosswalk light was blinking red. There were no oncoming cars. However, I reminded the boy of the red light. I waited patiently; but, the boy was anxious to cross the street.

After I finished the bank transactions, we went to a restaurant. The boy chose a sandwich and a free cup of water. When the boy finished eating, he went to the drink dispenser to refill with a soft drink. I told the boy he could refill with water but not a soft drink. I explained that he was stealing.

He agreed.

We walked back to the office and I reflected on the incidents.

I asked, "Am I that truthful? Am I that honest? Will I cross the pedestrian crosswalk when the signal light says 'Do Not Walk,' even though no cars are around?"

I took time to check my heart. I had a long way to go. However, this soul-searching time helped me know where I was.

Fifty stars

Tuesday arrived.

The election was three weeks away. I had to pick up precinct materials from the Office of Elections.

I offered the boy five dollars to carry a box of election materials back to the office.

The boy accepted the offer.

At the state's office, I opened the supply box, inspected the items, and checked the master list. I unfolded the United States flag and asked the boy how many stars were on the flag. He did not know, so, I asked him to count. He touched every star with his index finger.

After counting, he said, "Fifty."

Then, I asked him what those stars mean. He did not know. So, I explained each star represents a state. I gave him examples of Alaska, Texas, and Hawaii.

Later, I offered the boy two options to get back to the office. We could either catch the bus or walk back. I advised the boy that the cost of riding the bus was one dollar, which would be deducted from his five dollars.

The boy thought for a short moment. He wanted the full price. So, we walked.

I took out one hundred and fifty voter registration forms to lessen the weight of the box.

At 11:00 am, the day was warmer.

We stopped at a restaurant to purchase two cups of water. Then, we walked back to the office. At first, the boy possessed much energy and showed excitement. Then, the sun took its toll on the boy.

Trees cast shadows on the bike path and we each took refuge under the shades.

Then, we were three hundred yards away from the office. The park near the office was a familiar landmark. Before we went back to the office, we stopped to buy some more water.

Priceless gift

The time with the little boy offered priceless moments.

It brought back memories of times when I was young. The boy reminded me to be curious about simple things again.

How about you?

Are you curious about simple things?

Are you curious about what you can become?

The promise of life bursts like a morning sun when the mind is curious. Hope shines through the eyes of a little child.

Harvest the wisdom of the young ones. Enliven the simple things they share. When you see the simplicity of life, you begin to see it with freshness.

Do not go after trophies, applause, or accolades. Live to make someone smile. Do simple things to love yourself, others, and most of all God.

Do not go after fleeting glitter, but be in awe of the splendor of God. Live in the moment and the simplicity of today. The bigger things and tomorrow will take care of themselves.

"If any of you lacks wisdom, let him ask of God, who gives to all liberally and without reproach, and it will be given to him. But let him ask in faith, with no doubting, for he who doubts is like a wave of the sea driven and tossed by the wind. For let not that man suppose that we will receive anything from the Lord; he is a double-minded man, unstable in all his ways" (James 1:5-8).

QUESTIONS TO SEARCH YOUR SOUL

A. What are you doing with your time?

What are your major time wasters?
What are you doing about them?
What is the first step to be productive?

B. Daily life: *Unleash the Beauty and Power of Love* to your world

Create a caring place around your world.
Give praise to youths around you.
Pray for the people you talked with this week.

C. Self-discovery

Welcome each day like a child opening a gift on Christmas day.
Be curious about the simple things.
Every day, be ready for God-assigned moments.

15

Face of Life

Not knowing the face of life makes one wonder.
The day is bleak when the sun goes under.

All through the day and night, time slowly rests;
I learned faith is my light to receive God's best.

Life responds to the beckoning of my heart.
I will persevere to where love no longer parts.

Life has no meaning when there's no sacrifice;
A tender love makes obscure days nice.

Love is kind and never fails the Bible says;
I will be true to God so that love stays.

There is beauty and life in God's creation;
I choose to offer my heart with passion.

The moon smiled brighter when life came;
I will nurture and keep love burning aflame.

Seasons come. The cycles of life move on.
Love came and the Lord blessed under the sun.

Part Four

HEARTS GROWN COLD

CHECKLIST

Principles to instill

- History repeats itself. It is time to etch a unique story.
- If the church is not a preserving agent, what will become of the world?
- When you stand still, moments become clearer.

Things to do

- Share your goodness, not what destroys.
- Create a growing place for family, friends, and the world around you.
- Do not complain. Pick up the rubbish, put it in the garbage can, and move on.

A life to build

- Take family members to see a sunset.
- Share encouraging stories with friends and strangers.
- Create a growing place around you.

16

Microwave Oven Society

When we fail to follow God, we drift in a sea of confusion, struggle in the field of opportunity, and wither in the garden of life.

A counter cashier took my order.

It was her first day at the post. Actually, these were her first few hours taking orders, but she was poised to serve the hungry masses of humanity.

I asked for change in quarters so I could buy the Sunday paper. Then, I went to the newspaper stand fifteen feet away. I counted seven quarters twice before inserting the coins. I pulled the paper, turned around, and walked back to pick up my order. When I reached the counter, my food was ready.

I was not surprised.

It was the norm. It was expected.

While sitting in the restaurant, I thought about society speeding forward.

Then, it dawned on me. The likeness of society glowed before me in full view.

Two fathers sat twenty feet away. On the right, a father was huddled with three children.

On the left, six children surrounded a father. The farthest child looked like the oldest. The youngest sat next to the father. The dad went clockwise talking to the children and spent more time with the youngest and the girls. The oldest in the far corner sat quietly.

With excitement, the children ate their meals. They were happy.

Two dads spend time with their children offered priceless moments.

I wondered what road the children would take, what pains they would bear, and what triumphs they would harvest.

Moments later, I went back to the counter to find out how fast the food was prepared. An employee told me the restaurant instilled a self-imposed guideline to serve food in less than sixty seconds.

I went back to my table.

I pondered about the challenges of society. I reasoned the problem is not the fast-food industry. The problem is not modern gadgets. Technology in the twenty-first century serves society well. Yet, when technology is used without redeeming purpose, these gadgets drain promising lives. These tools bleed hopes, drown dreams, and waste precious time. We become slaves to technologies that were meant to give us more time and freedom.

When we fail to follow God, we drift in the sea of confusion, struggle in the field of opportunity, and wither in the garden of life. As a result, we live desperately in moments of plenty, become victims in a fast-paced world, and burn in the microwave oven society.

How about you?

Are you traveling in the fast lane?

Are you roasting in the oven of heated moments?

If you are, slow down to consider the life at hand and the journey before you. Take time to know yourself and take time to know God.

When you pause, you hear the heart speaking. When you stand still, moments become clearer. When the heart is humble, truth unfolds its secrets.

Faster, farther, and colder

The microwave oven was an invention of the twentieth century.[1]

In the 1945, a Raytheon engineer, with only a grade school education, found another use for radiation technology. Percy Spencer felt the candy bar in his pocket melt when exposed near a magnetron tube, a key part of the microwave radar.

In 1947, a microwave oven, called Radarange, was first built for commercial use. It stood six feet tall and weighed over seven hundred pounds. It cost over $2,000.

Then in 1967, Raytheon introduced a countertop model that cost around $500.

Over the years, the microwave oven gained popularity. Today, the microwave oven is a common feature in most kitchens.

With technology, we finish tasks faster.

A microwave oven cooks a meal in less than ten minutes. As a result, we should have more time for ourselves and for building relationships.

We live in a fast-moving society.

We rush to go somewhere and end up nowhere. As a result, we live in desperation. We run to the top hoping to find meaning. However, the top is empty. There is no peace and there is no contentment.

We rush all over the place and fail to see life. We lose direction and fail to see who we truly are. We deal with last-minute issues and do not have time to share our goodness. We do not see the blessings given, and we ignore simple joys in simple moments.

Society has grown cold.

Souls burn in the oven of pride, hearts sear in the heat of angry moments, and minds roast in the fire of hate.

In the process, we close our lives. We become strangers to ourselves. We move too quickly and lose the ability to connect with ourselves and others. We lose sight of the grand design of life. Many throw away moments that were meant to refresh the soul.

"But know this, that in the last days perilous times will come. For men will be lovers of themselves, lovers of money, boasters, proud, blasphemers, disobedient to parents, unthankful, unholy, unloving, unforgiving, slanderers, without self control, brutal, despisers of good, traitors, headstrong, haughty, lovers of pleasure rather lovers of God, having a form of godliness but denying its power. And from such people turn away!" (2 Tim. 3:1-5).

Without God, souls march forward to destruction.

Lives become restless and selfish. All search for meaning, look for love, and crave acceptance.

All along, peace, joy, love, and happiness have been in the background waiting. Sadly, wayward hearts have failed to sense them.

QUESTIONS TO SEARCH THE SOUL

A. Are you running in circles?

What are your priorities?
List them.
What are three important parts of your life?

B. Daily life: *Unleash the Beauty and Power of Love* to your family

Create a growing place for your family.
Take family members to see a sunset.
Pray for family members.

C. Self-discovery

What race are you running?
Are you going in circles without meaning?
Are you roasting in the oven of hate?

17

Lost Flavor

It starts with a simple compromise. The first deviation looks harmless. However, this deviousness grows like cancer and eats away any goodness within.

She turned her head.

The darkened life simmered in her heart. The worldly tentacles tied her soul to the city. She was cozy with the wickedness and wanted to go back.

The warning was given and the grace of God was upon Lot's wife and the city (Gen. 19).

Abraham asked God to spare Sodom. As a result, God told Abraham to find fifty upright people. Fifty people were not found. Abraham pleaded for forty-five. Forty-five were not found. Then, the count went down to forty, thirty, twenty, and ten--none were found.

The warning was ignored. Instead of repenting, the city reveled in sin. Sodom was destroyed and Lot's wife turned to salt.

In the end times, war, famine, pestilence, and hate take center stage. Good and evil clash and light and darkness collide.

Lawlessness runs amuck. Hearts grow cold, souls harden with pride, and many walk in wickedness.

The church was formed to show the love of God. However, man tainted it. As a result, many cannot find the love of God in places of worship.

In Revelation, six of the seven churches cast aside the ways of God.

It is a bleak reality.

The church dropped its desire to worship God, and as a result, the church gave away its power to be the salt of the earth (Mat. 5:13).

How then shall we conduct ourselves?

If the church is not a preserving agent, what then will become of the world?

What will become of society? What will become of us?

What will become of you?

End times

Revelation mentions seven churches.

Ruins of these first- and second-century churches show grim reminders of time passed.

Into which church do you fit? Which church reflects the condition of your heart?

Ephesus?	Left first love with Christ.
Smyrna?	Persecuted and blasphemed the church.
Pergamos?	Held the doctrine of Balaam and sexual immorality (Numbers 24, 25).
Thyatira?	Committed sexual immorality and ate food sacrificed to idols.
Sardis?	Did good works but was spiritually dead.
Philadelphia?	Overcame challenges and showed love.
Loadicea?	Lukewarm heart, neither hot nor cold.

Loveless church: Ephesus

"To the angel of the church in Ephesus write,
'These things says, He who holds the seven stars
in His right hand, who walks in the midst of the
seven golden lampstands: "I know your works, your
labor, your patience, and that you cannot bear those
who are evil. And you tested those who say they are
apostles and are not, and have found them liars; and
you have persevered and have patience, and have
labored for My name's sake and have not become
weary. Nevertheless I have this against you, that you
have left your first love. Remember therefore from
where you have fallen; repent and do the first works,
or else I will come to you quickly and remove your
lampstand from its place--unless you repent. But this
you have, that you hate the deeds of the Nicolaitans,
which I also hate.

"He who has an ear, let him hear what the Spirit
says to the churches. To him who overcomes I will
give to eat from the tree of life, which is in the midst
of the Paradise of God"" (Rev. 2:1-7).

Persecuted church: Smyrna

"And to the angel of the church in Smyrna write,
'These things says the First and Last, who
was dead, and came to life: "I know your works,
tribulation, and poverty (but you are rich); and I
know the blasphemy of those who say they are Jews
and are not, but are a synagogue of Satan. Do not
fear any of those things which you are about to suffer.
Indeed, the devil is about to throw some of you into
prison, that you may be tested, and you will have

tribulation ten days. Be faithful until death, and I will give you the crown of life.

"He who has an ear, let him hear what the Spirit says to the churches. He who overcomes shall not be hurt by the second death"'" (Rev. 2:8-11).

Compromising church: Pergamos

"And to the angel of the church in Pergamos write,

'These things says He who has the sharp two-edged sword: "'I know your works, and where you dwell, where Satan's throne is. And you hold fast to My name, and did not deny My faith even in the days even in the days in which Antipas was My faithful martyr, who was killed among you, where Satan dwells. But I have a few things against you, because you have there those who hold the doctrine of Balaam, who taught Balak to put a stumbling block before the children of Israel, to eat things sacrificed to idols, and to commit sexual immorality. Thus you also have those who hold the doctrine of the Nicolaitans, which thing I hate. Repent, or else I will come to you quickly and will fight against them with the sword of My mouth.

"He who has an ear, let him hear what the Spirit says to the churches. To him who overcomes I will give some of the hidden manna to eat. And I will give him a white stone, and on the stone a new name written which no one knows except him who receives it"'" (Rev. 2:12-17).

Corrupt church: Thyatira

"And the angel of the church of Thyatira write,
'These things says the Son of God, who has
eyes like a flame of fire, and His feet like fine brass:
"I know your works, love, service, faith, and your
patience; and as for your works, the last are more
than the first. Nevertheless I have a few things
against you, because you have allow that woman of
Jezebel, who calls herself a prophetess, to teach and
seduce My servants to commit sexual immorality
and to eat things sacrificed to idols. And I gave her
time to repent of her sexual immorality, and she
did not repent. Indeed I will cast her into a sickbed,
and those who commit adultery with her into great
tribulation, unless they repent of their deeds. I will
kill her children with death, and all the churches
shall know that I am He who searches the minds and
hearts. And I will give to each one of you according to
your works.

"Now to you I say, and to the rest in Thyatira,
as many as do not have this doctrine, who have not
know the depths of Satan, as they say, I will put on
you no other burden. But hold fast what you have till
I come. And he who overcomes, and keeps my word
My works until the end, to him I will give power over
the nations--

'He shall rule them with a rod of iron;
They shall be dashed to pieces like the potter's
vessels'--

as I also have received from My Father; and I will
give him the morning star.

"He who has an ear, let him hear what the Spirit
say to the churches""' (Rev. 2:18-29).

Dead church: Sardis

"And to the angel of the church in Sardis write,

'These things says He who has the seven Spirits of God and the seven stars: "I know your works, that you have a name that you are alive, but you are dead. Be watchful, and strengthen the things which remain, that are ready to die, for I have not found your works perfect before God. Remember therefore how you have received and heard; hold fast and repent. Therefore if you will not watch, I will come upon you as a thief, and you will not know what hour I will come upon you. You have a few names even in Sardis who have not defiled their garments; and they shall walk with Me in white, for they are worthy. He who overcomes shall be clothed in white garments, and I will not blot out his name from the Book of Life; but I will confess his name before My Father and before His angels.

"He who has an ear, let him hear what the Spirit says to the churches"'" (Rev. 3:1-6).

Faithful church: Philadelphia

"And to the angel of the church in Philadelphia write,

'These things says He who is holy, He who is true, "He who has the key of David, He who opens and no one shuts, and shuts and no one opens": "I know you works. See, I have set before you an open door, and no one can shut it; for you have a little strength, have kept My word, and have not denied My name. Indeed I will make those of the synagogue of Satan, who say they are Jews and are not, but lie--indeed I will

*make them come and worship before your feet, and
to know that I have loved you. Because you kept My
command to persevere, I also will keep you from the
hour of trial which shall come upon the whole world,
to test those who dwell on the earth. Behold, I am
coming quickly! Hold fast what you have, that no one
may take your crown. He who overcomes, I will make
him a pillar In the temple of My God, and he shall
go out no more. And I will write on him the name of
My God and the name of the city of My God, the New
Jerusalem, which comes down out of heaven from My
God. And I will write on him My new name.*

*"He who has an ear, let him hear what the Spirit
says to the churches""'* (Rev. 3:7-13).

Lukewarm church: Laodicea

*"And to the angel of the church of the Laodiceans
write,*

*'These things says the Amen, the Faithful and
True Witness, the Beginning of the creation of God: "I
know your works, that you are neither cold nor hot. I
could wish you were cold or hot. So then, because you
are lukewarm, and neither cold nor hot, I will vomit
you out of My mouth. Because you say, 'I am rich,
have become wealthy, and have need of nothing'--
and do not know that you are wretched, miserable,
poor, blind, and naked--I counsel you to buy from
Me gold refined in the fire, that you may be rich; and
white garments, that you may be clothed, that the
shame of your nakedness may not be revealed; and
anoint your eyes with eye salve, that you may see. As
many as I love, I rebuke and chasten. Therefore be
zealous and repent. Behold, I stand at the door and*

knock. If anyone hearts My voice and opens the door,
I will come in to him and dine with him, and he with
Me. To him who overcomes I will grant to sit with Me
on My throne, as I also overcame and sat down with
My Father on His throne.
"He who has an ear, let him hear what the Spirit
ways to the churches"" (Rev. 3:14-22).

One refill please . . .

The churches mentioned in Revelation started with a pure desire to worship God.

What happened?

If a church loses its desire to praise God, then it can happen to each one who believe and worship God.

It starts with a simple compromise. The first deviation looks harmless. Deceit grows like cancer and eats away any goodness within. It happens to all and can happen to you.

It happened to me.

A fast-food restaurant is located five hundred yards away from my office. For months, I went there at 5:45 am to read, to write, and to think.

When I first filled my cup, I noticed a sign above the dispenser that reads "One Refill Only." Every morning I bought a cup of iced tea.

During the first month, I complied with the one-refill policy. Other people refilled their cups three or four times. During that time, I questioned their uprightness.

Then, I caved in.

I reasoned that the cup was filled with ice and should be replaced with the same amount of iced tea. Weeks later, my conscience dulled and I refilled the cup two times.

At first, my conscience nudged my heart of the wrongdoing. As days passed, the guilt faded. I refilled my cup more than once and thought it was okay.

Then, I met an elderly woman working at the restaurant. Every morning, I saw her cleaning tables and mopping the floor. The frailty of her body made me pause.

From this encounter, conviction set in.

I repented and refilled my cup once.

When I am thirsty, I buy a larger cup.

This dark stain is washed away. I live with fewer burdens, less guilt, and less excess baggage latched onto my life.

I have long way to go. However, I conquered this battle and do not have to carry this guilt. Now, I refill once. I can live with that.

I am happy.

I am free!

QUESTIONS TO SEARCH YOUR SOUL

A. How is your character?

What is your report card in these categories?
Moral character? Inner voice? Helping others?
What are you doing to improve the person you are becoming?

B. Daily life: *Unleash the Beauty and Power of Love* to your friends

Create a growing place for friends.
Be a moral lighthouse for friends.
Share stories with moral lessons.

C. Self-discovery

Ask these questions: Am I a good person?
Am I moving towards the better me?
Am I leading people to better lives or worse?

18

America Buckles at Its Knees

The coming years expose the character of our nation.
Our actions define who we are and where we are going.
History serves us well. History provides grim reminders
of empires and people who came before us.

America buckles at its knees.

America fumbles its values and abandons its purpose. The nation strays away from its moral compass.

America started as a nation on its knees seeking God. On September 7, 1774, the first meeting of the Continental Congress was spent hours in prayer.[1]

The nation was founded on godly values. The Declaration of Independence, the Constitution, the government structure, and the court system were based on biblical principles. Most of the fifty-six signers were church members. Many delegates were pastors, deacons, and church leaders.

With hard work, they ushered a new nation forward. With trust in God, they forged a nation to greatness. As a result, America became a bastion of hope to millions.

Fifty-six men staked their families, honor, careers, and lives when they signed the Declaration of Independence. The youngest, at age twenty-six, was Edward Rutledge of South Carolina, and the oldest was Benjamin Franklin of Pennsylvania, at seventy. John Adams and Thomas Jefferson, who later became presidents, put their lives on the line.

Others put their lives on the battlefield and thousands shed their blood for the cause.

The Declaration of Independence revealed their lives, their stories, and their commitment.

Today, this document puts a magnifying glass on us to reveal our lives, our stories, and our dedication.

What will become of America? What will become of the world?

What will be our story?

Our voice

On July 4, 1776, the Declaration of Independence was first signed by John Hancock and later proclaimed to the world.[2]

This was the declaration of thirteen colonies to be called the United States of America.

This mandate projected the voices of patriots and God-fearing people yearning to be free from the tyranny of an oppressive government.

This is their life story.[3] This is their declaration:

> *When in the course of human Events, it becomes necessary for one People to dissolve the Political Bands which have connected them with another, and to assume among the Powers of the Earth, the separate and equal Station to which the Laws of Nature and of Nature's God entitle them, a decent Respect to the Opinions of Mankind requires that*

they should declare the causes which impel them to the Separation.

We hold these Truths to be self-evident, that all Men are created equal, that they are endowed by their Creator with certain unalienable Rights, that among these are Life, Liberty and the pursuit of Happiness--. That to secure these Rights, Governments are instituted among Men, deriving their just Powers from the Consent of the Governed, that whenever any Form of Government becomes destructive of these Ends, it is the Right of the People to alter or to abolish it, and to institute new Government, laying its Foundation on such Principles, and organizing its Powers in such Form, as to them shall seem most likely to effect their Safety and Happiness. Prudence, indeed, will dictate that Governments long established should not be changed for light and transient Causes; and accordingly all Experience hath shewn, that Mankind are more disposed to suffer, while Evils are sufferable, than to right themselves by abolishing the Forms to which they are accustomed. But when a long Train of Abuses and Usurpations, pursuing invariably the same Object, evinces a Design to reduce them under absolute Despotism, it is their Right, it is their Duty, to throw off such Government, and to provide new Guards for their future Security. Such has been the patient Sufferance of these Colonies; and such is now the Necessity which constrains them to alter their former Systems of Government. The History of the Present King of Great-Britain is a History of repeated Injuries and Usurpations, all having in direct Object the Establishment of an absolute Tyranny over these

States. To prove this, let Facts be submitted to a candid World.

He has refused his Assent to Laws, the most wholesome and necessary for the public Good.

He has forbidden his Governors to pass Laws of immediate and pressing importance, unless suspended in their Operation till his Assent should be obtained; and when so suspended, he has utterly neglected to attend to them.

He has refused to pass other Laws for the Accommodation of large Districts of People; unless those People would relinquish the Right of Representation in the Legislature, a Right inestimable to them, and formidable to Tyrants only.

He has called together Legislative Bodies at Places unusual, uncomfortable, and distant from the Depository of their public Records, for the sole Purpose of fatiguing them into Compliance with his Measures.

He has dissolved Representative Houses repeatedly, for opposing with manly Firmness his Invasions on the Rights of the People.

He has refused for a long Time, after such Dissolutions, to cause others to be elected; whereby the Legislative Powers, incapable of Annihilation, have returned to the People at large for their exercise; the State remaining in the mean time exposed to all the Dangers of Invasion from without, and Convulsions within.

He has endeavoured to prevent the Population of these States; for that Purpose obstructing the Laws for Naturalization of Foreigners; refusing to pass others to encourage their Migrations hither, and raising the Conditions of new Appropriations of Lands.

He has obstructed the Administration of Justice, by refusing his Assent to Laws for establishing Judiciary Powers.

He has made Judges dependent on his Will alone, for the Tenure of their Offices, and Amount and Payment of their Salaries

He has erected a Multitude of new Offices, and sent hither Swarms of Officers to harass our People, and eat out their Substance.

He has kept among us, in Times of Peace, Standing Armies, without the consent of our Legislature.

He has affected to render the Military independent of and superior to the Civil Power.

He has combined with others to subject us to a Jurisdiction foreign to our Constitution, and unacknowledged by our Laws; giving his Assent to their Acts of pretended Legislation:

For quartering large Bodies of Armed Troops among us:

For protecting them, by a mock Trial, from Punishment for any Murders which they should commit on the Inhabitants of these States:

For cutting off our Trade with all Parts of the World:

For imposing taxes on us without our Consent:

For depriving us, in many Cases, of the Benefits of Trial by Jury:

For transporting us beyond Seas to be tried for pretended Offences:

For abolishing the free System of English Laws in a neighbouring Province, establishing therein an arbitrary Government, and enlarging its Boundaries, so as to render it at once an Example and fit instrument for introducing the same absolute Rule in these Colonies:

For taking away our Charters, abolishing our most valuable Laws, and altering fundamentally the Forms of our Governments:

For suspending our own Legislatures, and declaring themselves invested with Powers to legislate for us in all Cases whatsoever.

He has abdicated Government here, by declaring us out of his Protection and waging War against us.

He has plundered our Seas, ravaged our Coasts, burnt our Towns, and destroyed the Lives of our People.

He is, at this Time, transporting large Armies of foreign Mercenaries to compleat the Works of Death, Desolation, and Tyranny, already begun with circumstances of Cruelty and Perfidy, scarcely paralleled in the most barbarous Ages, and totally unworthy the Head of a civilized Nation.

He has constrained our fellow Citizens taken Captive on the high Seas to bear Arms against their Country, to become the Executioners of their Friends and Brethren, or to fall themselves by their Hands.

He has excited domestic Insurrections among us, and has endeavoured to bring on the Inhabitants of our Frontiers, the merciless Indian Savages, whose known Rule of Warfare, is an undistinguished Destruction of all Ages, Sexes and Conditions.

In every stage of these Oppressions we have Petitioned for Redress in the most humble Terms:

Our repeated Petitions have been answered only by repeated injury. A Prince, whose Character is thus marked by every act which may define a Tyrant, is unfit to be the Ruler of a free People.

Nor have we been wanting in Attentions to our British Brethren. We have warned them from Time to Time of Attempts by their Legislature to extend an unwarrantable Jurisdiction over us. We have reminded them of the Circumstances of our Emigration and Settlement here. We have appealed to their native Justice and Magnanimity, and we have conjured them by the Ties of our common Kindred to disavow these Usurpations, which, would inevitably interrupt our Connections and Correspondence. They too have been deaf to the Voice of Justice and of Consanguinity. We must, therefore, acquiesce in the Necessity, which denounces our Separation, and hold them, as we hold the rest of Mankind, Enemies in War, in Peace, Friends.

We, therefore, the Representatives of the UNITED STATES OF AMERICA, in GENERAL CONGRESS, Assembled, appealing to the Supreme Judge of the World for the Rectitude of our intentions, do, in the Name, and by the Authority of the good People of these Colonies, solemnly Publish and Declare, That these United Colonies are, and of Right ought to be, FREE AND INDEPENDENT STATES; that they are absolved from all Allegiance to the British Crown, and that all political Connection between them and the State of Great-Britain, is and ought to be totally dissolved; and that as FREE AND INDEPENDENT STATES, they have full Power to levy War, conclude Peace, contract Alliances, establish Commerce, and

to do all other Acts and Things which INDEPENDENT
STATES *may of right do.* **And for the support of**
this Declaration, with a firm Reliance on the
Protection of divine Providence, we mutually
pledge to each other our Lives, our Fortunes, and
our sacred Honor.

Many sacrificed their lives to birth a nation.

Now, we need the same sacrifice to keep America moving forward.

The coming years expose our character. Our actions define us. Also, our actions will define our nation and its trajectory.

History serves us well.

It provides grim reminders of empires and people that came before us.

God raises kingdoms and takes down nations. God raises people and takes down leaders.

We receive glimpses of the future by looking at the past. For those who live after us, our actions become their history.

From this moment on, we need protection and guidance from the Almighty. Once again, we need to *"pledge our lives, our fortunes, and our sacred honor"* to move the nation forward. Our commitment to this cause sets the tone for our society. Our commitment dictates whether or not children will enjoy the same bounties we take for granted.

Ray of hope

America is not alone.

The world is getting darker. Like Sodom and Gomorrah, the warning has been given. The destruction of wicked hearts comes at an appointed time.

However, there is hope.

God says, *"If My people who are called by My name will humble themselves, and pray and seek My face, and turn from their wicked ways, then I will hear from heaven, and will forgive their sin and heal their land"* (2 Chron. 7:14).

During moments of turmoil, truth shines as beacon of light to guide souls out of darkness. Love's purity calms hearts during testing times. God will be there to guide. God will be there to intervene. God will be there to give strength to those who call upon Him.

What will you do? What can you do?

One person can turn a nation around. One person can influence the world.

Our choices determine our destiny as a people and as a nation.

Let us share our goodness with others, not the hate that destroys us.

Let us work to brighten moments, not stew on failures.

Let us do what we can today, not dream about tomorrow.

Most of all let us look to God, the Author and Finisher of our lives.

QUESTIONS TO SEARCH YOUR SOUL

A. What can you do to better society?

Write down the plan.
Start with simple ideas. Share them.
Start working on those ideas.

B. Daily life: *Unleash the Beauty and Power of Love* to your neighbors

Create a growing place with neighbors.
Grow relationships by getting to know the people around you.
Do not complain. Pick up the rubbish, put it in the garbage can, and move on.

C. Self-discovery

If the house is burning, what do you do?
If life is burdened, what do you do?
What is your first step? What is you second step?

19

Will the Real Leader Please Stand Up?

*Simple acts of kindness add up. The smile we share
lifts souls stuck in the gutter. Encouragement ignites
shattered dreams ready to be snuffed out.*

The challenge is apparent.

People trample each other and nations fight against nations.

Hate is spewed like molten lava. It comes out hot, caustic, and deadly. It burns bridges of hope, blots out peace, and destroys life.

Hate spreads to families, cities, and nations. Moral decay drowns promising lives. As a result, we become strangers to neighbors, move away from one another, and ignore hurting souls around us. At the same time, we ignore the pains inside.

More than ever, we need leaders. We need leaders to ignite the torch of faith. More than ever, we need leaders to uphold truth and ignite passion to care, to share, and to love.

Leaders live among us. They are in our midst.

The leaders amongst us are you and me.

We bear the task to better society. We bear the task of helping one another.

It starts with you.

It starts with me. It starts with all of us.

We can make a difference. Each simple smile, each gentle kindness, and each token of love strung together can transform the world.

Peace of our time

History provides lessons for the living.

The Munich Pact was signed on September 30, 1938. England, France, Italy, and Hitler's Germany agreed to the peace plan.

After signing the treaty, the Prime Minister of Great Britain went back to London to boast the Munich Pact to the people. He proclaimed the agreement as the "peace in our time" treaty.

Sadly, no one stopped the aggression of Hitler as he occupied Sudetenland. The allies did not help Czechoslovakia. As a result, Hitler seized Czechoslovakia.

Twelve months after signing the treaty, the turmoil flared into one of the bloodiest wars in history.

At the start of the millennium, conflicts explode across the globe. Turmoil flares in Africa, the Americas, Asia, Europe, the Middle East, and countries in the former Soviet Union. If we fail to stamp out these conflicts, they will become raging battles, destroying lives, cities, and nations.

If we cry "peace" as a solution to these conflicts, we are in for a surprise. Problems will not go away. As hearts of men become darker, global turmoil will get worse.

Lessons from the past provide clues. The past sheds light on the future. However, we ignore the wisdom of the past. We repeat same mistakes and allow history to repeat itself.

Today, leaders wave "the peace of our time" flag as horrific signs speak boldly.

Do we need another calamity to wake us up?

In 1993, terrorists attempted to topple the World Trade Center. They failed. Then, we sat back in complacency.

The Cobalt towers and the USS Cole were bombed. On 9/11, terrorists attacked the World Trade Center again. This time, the twin towers came down. Thousands died.

Spotlight on you

Leaders in the spotlight do their best.

However, I, you, and all of us need to stand up. We cannot sit back and watch. There is so much in the balance--our lives, our families, and our world.

Society needs you. However big or small, a simple act of love makes a difference. We need to get involved. We need to do our share.

We need caring moms to comfort crying children showered with hate. We need fathers to teach boys fairness in the ball field of life. We need people to carry the torch of love, and proclaim truth as the social order veers into lawlessness.

Simple acts of kindness add up.

The smile you share lifts a soul stuck in the gutter. Encouragement ignites a shattered dream ready to be snuffed out.

You never know who receives the kindness.

The good tidings you share come back in good measure to warm your soul.

Chapter 19: **Will the Real Leader Please Stand Up?**

QUESTIONS TO SEARCH YOUR SOUL

A. What major issues do you see around your world?

What are your solutions?
What are you doing about it?
What are you doing about it today?

B. Daily life: *Unleash the Beauty and Power of Love* to the world

Create a growing place around you.
Build people's confidence.
Help them conquer their challenges.

C. Self-discovery

Do you watch the world pass by?
Do you sit back as others take action?
What can you do today to make a difference?

20

Just Me, the Voice Crying Within

II

You were young, lived for selfish moments, and
death knocked many times and you did not know.

You enjoyed morsels of life, you craved more,
you wanted them now so you sold your tomorrow.

You filled your heart with dreams and aspirations
and so you boldly go to where your heart's desired.

You said, "I can conquer the world" and you had
so much energy so kept going until the heart tired.

There were ups and downs in each season of
life and you go after short-lived events.

You tried to live a life, however, there
were painful hurts and lonely moments.

You went through storms, you lived a life,
and you had no spirit, no fun under the sun.

You paused for a short fleeting moment but
failed to ask God how life should be done.

Part Five

TOOLS OF LIFE

Part Five: **Tools of Life**

CHECKLIST

Principles to instill

- Look straight ahead. Looking sideways proves costly.

- God is the Giver of life and the Giver of days.

- As you embrace the love of God, you will find life.

Things to do

- Spend daily time to know the person inside.

- Use productive words every time.

- Create a helping place for family, friends, and neighbors.

A life to build

- Praise people. Seek the good in others.

- Call a friend to get together for lunch or dinner.

- Smile at people. Laugh at yourself.

21

Lean Inward

*We hide inside shells of denials and go under
shades of lies to avoid piercing rays of truth.*

W hen I was in high school, my track coach said, "Lean
inward, stay focus, and give it all you have. At the turn, let your
momentum help push you forward."

He further advised me, "If you practice hard and do your best,
you will do fine."

Little did I know at that time that this advice also applies to
life.

To run the race of life, you lean inward, stay focused, give it
your all, and let your victories and defeats push you forward.

Life is an ongoing process of leaning forward, committing
dreams to action, and engaging the heart to challenges at hand.

Each day, look inward. Focus on what is before you and lean
toward God.

Looking back proves costly.

Turning sideways takes you out of the game. A split second
glance may be the time needed to win the race.

By the same token, looking at failures takes the soul out of an unfolding life.

There is no magic formula to life.

There is no secret potion to love.

There is no secret path to happiness.

It boils down to putting your heart on the line to *Unleash the Beauty and Power of Love.* Look inward, take simple steps forward, and walk with God.

When you are determined, the world makes room for you. When you persevere, the path becomes distinct. When you are proven, you come out glowing.

". . . Let us lay aside every weight, and the sin which so easily ensnares us, and let us run with endurance the race that is set before us, looking unto Jesus, the Author and Finisher of our faith, who for the joy that was set before Him endured the cross, despising the shame, and has sat down at the right hand of the throne of God" (Heb. 12:1, 2).

How about you?

Are you leaning forward?

Are you looking unto Jesus?

Sadly, many hide in the shadows of yesterday and lean backward. They lock their lives in the past and throw ashes of yesterday on themselves over and over. If you allow them, they will throw their ashes on you, too.

Guardrails of truth

Each day, we try to usher brighter moments.

However, dreams are jailed behind bars of fear. We bring out longings to please wild desires. We try many roads, seek many avenues, and walk on many paths. Yet, our solutions fall short of the joy we yearn to possess.

We scatter hope, but come up empty. We chase wild cravings, but end up with nothing.

H. C. Villanueva

We miss the path to life and cease to grasp what we can become. In the process, we drop dreams, mangle inspirations, and taint imaginations.

We are afraid to look at the darkness of our soul. We are afraid to confront our frailties. Many avoid the truth and many avoid life's pruning and refining process. Instead, we chose our desired path and we start all over again at a lower lever.

You decide how life unfolds.

You decide what comes out of your life.

Testing bares the soul. Hardships refine the heart. Perseverance polishes life, rounding sharp corners and smoothing rough moral character.

Gold, like life, goes through a refining process.

The gold is found. Mined. Crushed. Gold particles are placed in the furnace to remove impurities. Heat brings out the gold's beauty.

Likewise, life is tested by adversity, distilled by misfortune, and transformed by God.

Heated moments expose impurities settled in the soul.

The fire of adversity brings out the beauty of the soul and dark stains of the heart.

When you allow God to refine you, you come out gleaming no matter the circumstance.

Each day, search your soul.

Know who you are, where you are going, and what you are becoming.

Protect your heart by putting up guardrails of truth. Fill your mind with the Word of God. Memorize Bible verses, let the Word of God touch your soul, and allow the Word to guide you each day.

"Let not mercy and truth forsake you; bind them around your neck, write them on the tablet of your heart, and so find favor and high esteem in the sight of God and man" (Prov. 3:3, 4).

When you protect your heart, you use less time mending a broken soul. When you give your heart to God, He softens a hardened soul and cleanses a tainted life.

Chapter 21: **Lean Inward**

QUESTIONS TO SEARCH YOUR SOUL

A. What do you see within?

> Is there pain, a dark past, or failure?
> Is there joy, peace, or love?
> Find peace in God, love in sadness, and joy in hurt.

B. Daily life: *Unleash the Beauty and Power of Love* to your family

> Create a helping place for your family.
> Listen to the heartbeats of your family members.
> Praise each family member every day.

C. Self-discovery

> Listen to the voice within.
> What do you hear?
> See the good in everything.

H. C. Villanueva

22

Childlike Curiosity

There will always be a child in you. Harness the power of a childlike heart. Be simple. Be curious, be humble, and be willing to learn.

The elephant reigns as the largest land mammal.

Some Savanna Elephants grow over thirteen feet tall and weigh over 15,000 pounds.

At birth, an elephant calf weighs between 200 and 300 pounds and gains about two pounds per day. Eventually, it grows to be a gentle giant in the wild but ferocious when provoked.

Trainers use a unique method of subduing this giant. They take a young elephant and tie one end of a rope to its leg and the other end to a stake. At first, the baby elephant tries to break the rope.

It tugs.

It wiggles.

It complains.

Day after day, the young elephant tries to break free. After failed attempts, the elephant confines itself to the length of the rope. The elephant stops trying and becomes comfortable being tied up.

Years later, the adult elephant weighs couple of tons. Trainers tie a small rope to a much larger elephant. When the elephant feels a tug, it stops and retreats.

After years of confinement, a self-limiting mind-set is ingrained in the creature. The conditioned mind forbids the giant creature from attempting to break out of its bondage.

The creature is confined in an "elephant trap."

How about you?

Are you in a self-limiting trap?

As adults, fear limits the mind. Failure, hurt, and pain drown dreams, aspirations, and plans. Fear locks the feet from moving forward. Mental blocks tie the heart to a mediocre level.

At birth, our minds were bare with experience but simple, open, and curious.

As we grew, we painted the canvas of our soul with dreams, ideals, and plans. Also, we etched hurt, pain, and failure on our hearts.

As a child, we had a curious mind. At a young age, we gathered simple knowledge and possessed energy to know the world. We fired a barrage of questions to soothe youthful interest.

Then, we experienced failures.

As time passed and we experienced setbacks, we slowed down to gain knowledge. We abandoned the childlike curiosity. As a result, a promising life stopped growing and we lose the zest to live.

What happened to many of us?

We stopped asking questions. We now ignore simple things that provide depth to our lives.

Open book

The past is either a blessing or a curse.

Bad memories pull the soul down. On the other hand, the past can serve as a road sign reminding the heart to take a wiser route the next time around.

H. C. Villanueva

When you see the past as a wise teacher, you are ready to tackle the challenges of today. When you know today is a gift, you welcome the ranging demands of living. When you realize God holds your tomorrow, you forge forward to face today.

The Bible says, *"You are our epistle written in our hearts, known and read by all men, clearly you are an epistle of Christ, ministered by us, written not with ink by the Spirit of the living God, not on tablets of stone but on tablets of flesh, that is, of the heart"* (2 Cor. 3:2, 3).

Life is like a book.

You open a book to see its contents. You read the chapters, paragraphs, and sentences to know its message. You ponder the words to bare its essence.

Likewise, you open your life to others to reveal the content of the soul. You etch noble essence on the lives of people by sharing your kindness.

Do not hesitate to share your life today. Do not hold back today's blessings for tomorrow.

Do not let past pains hinder you from receiving today's gift. Do not let darkened experiences lock you in despair. Do not let past pains stop you from sharing your life. Do not let past failures stop you from living a full life.

"Of a sound mind"

When I was in high school, I tipped a glass from a kitchen counter. As I tried to save the glass from falling, I leaned forward against the side of the counter and hit the glass. It broke and cut a one-inch gash on my index finger.

Thereafter, suicidal thoughts tortured my mind. When I saw a glass, my mind gravitates toward it with a strong ensuing desire to be cut.

For many years, this thought tortured my mind.

Then, I searched for an answer to deal with this suicidal urge.

The Word of God was the solution to beat this dark thought. When the thought began to creep into my mind, I recited a Bible verse to jar the notion from building up in my mind. I said, *"For God has not given us a spirit of fear, but of power and of love and of a sound mind"* (2 Tim 1:7).

"For God has not given us a spirit of fear, but of power and of love and of a sound mind" (2 Tim 1:7).

After repeating the verse several times, the suicidal thought faded away.

It worked. The word of God saved the day. The Word of God saved my life.

Jesus said, *"You search the Scriptures, for in them you think you have eternal life; and these are they which testify of Me"* (John 5:39).

Search the Word of God. Seek the Giver of life.

Seek to live brighter moments. Do not waste precious time moaning over failed efforts. Do not waste energy simmering over past problems. Look to God, learn the lessons, and move on.

Have a childlike heart. See the richness of children's hearts. Their tender hearts shine bright lights on darkened souls draped with fear, hurt, and pain. Young ones help us see the simple things we left behind.

Harness the power of what a childlike heart brings. Be simple. Be curious, humble, and willing to learn. Be naive enough to be curious. Be eager to take the first step, and be bold to open the door.

Chapter 22: **Childlike Curiosity**

QUESTIONS TO SEARCH YOUR SOUL

A. Do you have a childlike curiosity?

What makes you curious?
Begin to answer: What? Why? How?
What were your childhood dreams?

B. Daily life: *Unleash the Beauty and Power of Love* to your friends

Create a helping place for friends.
Call a friend and get together for lunch or dinner.
Pray for your friends.

C. Self-discovery

What dreams do you want to accomplish?
Take time to watch children playing.
Ignite the passion to learn the simple things of life.

23

Your Words

Words determine your destiny, your future, and your today. Words are seedlings to life. What you say today will bear fruit tomorrow.

The sun still hid behind the eastern horizon and the haste of humanity had not yet stirred the virgin morning.

Slowly, thirty souls huddled under a dimly lit park pavilion.

At 6 am, we began our exercise.

One morning, I came ten minutes early. Kaz, an elderly man, arrived early, too.[1]

I had met Kaz three weeks earlier and told him about a writing project.

Right away, he encouraged me. During the following weeks, he asked about my progress. Then, he shared news of my plan with others.

As weeks passed, he encouraged me and lavished me with praises.

Did he discern something I did not know?

Did he discern something about my future?

Maybe he knew these Bible verses: *"A word fitly spoken is like apples of gold in settings of silver"* (Prov. 25:11).

"Death and life are in the power of the tongue, and those who love it will eat its fruit" (Prov. 18:21).

"For by your words you will be justified, and by your words you will be condemned" (Matt. 12:37).

I welcomed Kaz's optimism.

Each Monday morning, I look forward waking up at 5 am, for I know I will be uplifted.

Speak life

Imagine, waking up one morning and saying, "I feel sick. It is going to be a lousy day."

Gloomy thoughts wrap around your soul. You see yourself in the mirror. Wrinkles are magnified, defeat shows itself, and the ugliness of life rears its head.

You pause for a moment. You do not to see good within and do not pause long enough to see the beauty inside. You step out to meet the world.

Then, somebody asks, "How are you doing?"

A flood of thoughts rushes through your mind. Then, you repeat the sad music you have been singing. You reveal what is wrong with you, expose what is wrong with people, and share what is wrong with the world.

You say it with conviction because you sang the mantra many times before.

"A man's stomach shall be satisfied from the fruit of his mouth; from the produce of his lips he shall be filled. Death and life are in the power of the tongue, and those who love it will eat its fruit" (Prov. 18:20, 21).

You chose how you view your situations. And you choose how you live your life.

When you wake up, you have a choice.

You can be sad or happy.

Say, *"LORD, make me to know my end, and what is the measure of my days, that I may know how frail I am"* (Ps. 39:4).

The day may be dreary and the situation may be gloomy. However, you have a choice to let hope shine in and through your life.

Say, "This is the day the LORD has made; we will rejoice and be glad in it" (Ps. 118:24).

Your words create motion. Your words are your life.

You speak into existence the person you are today.

Words determine your today, your future, and your destiny. Words are seedlings to life. What you say today will bear fruit tomorrow.

Imagine if every word bubbling in your soul came true.

Imagine what you can become when you speak life, health, hope, and God's truth. Instead of repeating problems, imagine what happens when you speak solutions, optimism, and love.

Imagine what happens when you speak the Word of God.

"All flesh is as grass, and all the glory of man as the flower of the grass. The grass withers, and its flowers falls away, but the word of the LORD endures forever . . ." (1 Pet. 1:24, 25).

QUESTIONS TO SEARCH YOUR SOUL

A. Imagine what you can become when you speak of faith, hope, and life.

> Give words of praise to five people each day.
> Are you optimistic? Or are you pessimistic?
> Always be prepared to share something good, positive, or uplifting.

B. Daily life: *Unleash the Beauty and Power of Love* to your neighbors

> Create a helping place for neighbors.
> Praise your neighbors.
> Make it a habit to share good things.

C. Self-discovery

> Monitor what you are saying to yourself.
> Put words to productive use every day.
> Recite a Bible verse when tempted with negative thought.

24

Door to Realization

There is no defeat when you grow from failures.
There is no failure when you try your best.

Solomon opened his past for us to see.

He shared timeless truths that a life without God is vain, empty, and fruitless. He wrote, *"Vanity of vanities, all is vanity"* (Eccles. 1:2b).

During his prime years, Solomon ventured to find meaning and purpose. He tried wisdom. Kings and queens marveled at his words.

He tried earthly possessions. Solomon amassed wealth, but warned about building vast fortunes.

He said, *"Then I hated all my labor in which I had toiled under the sun, because I must leave it to the man who will come after me. And who knows whether he will be wise or a fool? Yet he will rule over all my labor in which I toiled and in which I have shown myself wise under the sun. This also is vanity"* (Eccles. 2:18, 19).

Reflecting during his old age, he said a life without God is empty (Ecclesiastes 1-12).

When life hits bottom, what do you do?

Heed Solomon's advice. Pause. Go to God.

Take time outs. Rest your mind. The waiting period helps secure much-needed rest for a tired soul.

During a time-out, see the situation, survey your surroundings, and look to God.

Fourth Commandment

"Remember the Sabbath day, to keep it holy. Six days you shall labor and do all your work, but the seventh day is the Sabbath of the LORD your God. In it you shall do no work: you, nor your son, nor your daughter, nor your male servant, nor your female servant, nor your cattle, nor your stranger who is within your gates. For in six day the LORD made the heavens and the earth, the sea, and all that is in them, and rested the seventh day. Therefore the LORD blessed the Sabbath day and hallowed it" (Exod. 20:8-11).

Rest one day a week.

Make time for yourself. Observe the nuances of life. Look toward heaven, grab the hands of God, and see your life ready to be unleashed.

Spend time with your dreams.

Polish noble ideas.

Make plans simple and plain.

Keep trying, keep growing, and keep on believing. Each day, work on your life.

There is no defeat when you grow from failure. There is no failure when you tried your best.

Work on your dreams, not envying others' success.

Work on your aspirations, not dwelling on past mistakes.

Work on your character, not layering your heart with hurts.

Work on your plans, not comparing your life with others.

Work on your life, for it is a gift from God.

As godly deeds move your heart, share them, live them, and do them. As you spend quiet moments, dreams become clearer and hope becomes stronger.

Red carpet

Defeats have their shining moments.

Allow failures to tutor you. Failures have priceless lessons to share. Setbacks are part of life. Turn defeats into spices of life to add flavor to your soul. Turn letdowns of life into heirlooms for others to harness the beauty and power of the lessons.

Do not waste moments swimming in regret. Rise up from the murky pool of defeat. See the priceless lessons placed on rocky situations.

Learn from people.

Listen to their soul tempered by failure. Learn from their mistakes, observe their follies, and heed their warnings. When you listen, it saves you years of pain, prevents needless hurt, and helps avoid many agonies.

Do not travel the same troubled road. Do not repeat the same mistakes. Heed the wisdom placed before you.

Let the Word of God guide you. *"For the word of God is living and powerful, and sharper than any two-edged sword, piercing even to the division of soul and spirit, and of joints and marrow, and is a discerner of the thoughts and intents of the heart"* (Heb. 4:12).

QUESTIONS TO SEARCH YOUR SOUL

A. Do you have a time to pause your routine?

Plan a time out each week.
Spend four hours this week thinking about life, dreams, and plans.
Ask the question: How am I doing with my life?

B. Daily life: *Unleash the Beauty and Power of Love* to your world

Create a helping place for your world.
Read the life story of Solomon, David, apostle Paul, etc.
Share their life stories with friends.

C. Self-discovery

When you have a challenge, what do you do first?
When in the midst of confusion, what is your first step?
Speak solutions. Do not recite problems.

H. C. Villanueva

25

Just Me, the Voice Crying Within
III

You hoard power, fame, and pride; your spirit
was high and you failed to get on your knees.

You had a grand ball, everybody was there
and I was a lone stranger among guests.

Now you walk slower, wrinkles etched deeper,
lungs breathe slower, and you try to look your best.

Regrets, disappointments burn in your soul and say,
"Oh, How I wish I want to do better than the rest."

You wonder how the days, the months, the years
and your life faded away from your presence.

The excitement, the laughter, and pleasure were fun
for a season but lost their glitter and essence.

You were on your deathbed, many came to
say their last goodbye; all left except me.

You were befuddled why I was standing
there alone with thee; I said, "You are me."

Part Six

LIFE UNDER THE SUN

CHECKLIST

Principles to instill

- Small acts strung together create a life.
- Move dreams forward with simple steps.
- Opportunities come to all. You have a choice to grab them.

Things to do

- Take an outing each week to see the wonders of creation.
- Create a nurturing place for family, friends, and neighbors.
- Set aside twenty minutes each day polishing noble ideas.

A life to build

- Find three people willing to learn and grow with you.
- Take time to know people's dreams and their journey.
- Do simple acts of kindness each day.

26

Make a Ripple

*The heart is your life bank vault. It accepts all
currencies of life. It accepts hurt, pain, and failure.
It also accepts joy, peace, and love. Later, you can
withdraw what you put in, plus a little bit more.*

A pond remains calm under a peaceful morning.

Throw a stone into a serene water and see what happens. The
rock creates ripples and impacts the whole body of water.

Throw a noble dream into a pool of ideas. See what happens.
The idea creates ripples in the marketplace of creativity.

Cast a life into the sea of humanity.

See what happens.

The life creates ripples in the hearts of people.

Cast your heart to the hands of God and see what happens.
Heaven rejoices and your soul will find life.

Take a humble soul and mold it, nurture it, and share it.

See what happens.

In the beginning, opportunity favors no one. In the end,
triumph surrounds itself with those who persevered.

Life is not an accident. It is a gift from God. However, you must make a conscious effort to live it. Most of all, you must make a conscious effort to build the life you have been given.

Pursue simple moments, accept simple joys, and cherish simple victories.

Each moment, good or bad, opens a door to something remarkable.

Each moment, focus on the task at hand.

Free the mind from worry. Worrying does not change the situation. Worrying adds more problems and more stress. Worrying steals the joy, the peace, and the love in your soul.

"*Therefore do not worry about tomorrow, for tomorrow will worry about its own things. Sufficient for the day is its own trouble*" (Matt. 6:34).

Life is tested in the oven of hardship. Take heart when defeat drowns the soul. Take heart when you are alone. In due course, you come out polished. In due time, you move forward.

The heart is your life bank vault. It accepts all currencies of life. It accepts hurt, pain, and failure. It also accepts joy, peace, and love. Later you can withdraw what you put in plus a little bit more.

Budding ideas

The Golden Arches began its humble beginning in San Bernardino, California.[1]

In 1948, Richard and Maurice McDonald changed their barbecue drive-in stand into the world's first McDonald's. The restaurant offered a limited menu around burgers, fries, and soft drinks.

Customers flocked to the restaurant.

On the other hand, the late wind of success favored a traveling salesman.

He was fifty-two years old.

The travel across America opened his eyes. Arduous years toughened his resolved and decades of experience enlarged his vision.

The man was Ray Kroc.

Ray Kroc made gut-wrenching decisions. He signed a mortgage loan to cash out the equity of his house, took money from his savings, and bought a distributorship to sell the Multimixer, a five-spindled milkshake maker.

During a sales visit, a lone San Bernardino fast-food stand that bought eight Multimixers piqued Ray Kroc's attention. At that moment, Ray Kroc grabbed the opportunity.

In 1954, Ray Kroc bought a franchising right from the McDonald brothers.

In 1955, he opened a McDonald's restaurant in Des Plaines, Illinois.

Today, the restaurant evolved into McDonald's Corporation with over thirty-two thousand restaurants in over one hundred countries.

Currency of life

Life is a journey of inner discovery.

Life is a journey of meeting opportunities and collecting memories.

Life also is a journey of seeking God.

Sadly, many look outside the soul and away from God.

Many have not figured out the depth of life or the potentials God has placed in each soul.

"For we are His workmanship, created in Christ Jesus for good works, which God prepared beforehand that we should walk in them" (Eph. 2:10).

The gifts God placed in the soul have not been fathomed or harnessed.

We have yet to unleash the power God has placed in us. Joshua asked God to make the earth stand still, Moses asked God to part the Red Sea, and David asked God to bring down the giant.

How about you?

What have you been asking God?

Chapter 26: **Make a Ripple**

QUESTIONS TO SEARCH YOUR SOUL

A. What is your life mission?

Name five things that are important to you.
What have you been doing about them lately?
What are you doing to improve them today?

B. Daily life: *Unleash the Beauty and Power of Love* to your family

Create a nurturing place for family.
Take a family outing to help the needy.
Each day, pray for each family member.

C. Self-discovery

Dreams fuel the soul to move you forward.
Rekindle youthful dreams.
Find the simple things of life.

27

Power of Faith

In the face of adversity, you are forced to define yourself.
You are given a chance to show your essence. The depth of
your heart is exposed and the size of your faith is revealed.

Mount Everest rises 29,035 feet high toward the heavens.

It is huge, beautiful, and majestic.

In 1841, Sir George Everest, the British Surveyor General of India, recorded the location of this mountain.

Since 1922, more than four thousand groups have attempted to climb this mountain.

In the process, over two hundred souls have succumbed to their death.

Attempts to climb Mount Everest are increasing. At the same time, more lives face death.

How about you?

Do you have a mountain to climb?

Are you willing to take the risk?

Are you willing to take an uphill journey?

In the face of adversity, you are forced to define yourself. You are given a chance to show your essence. The depth of your heart is exposed and the size of your faith is revealed.

Mountains of life expose who you are.

Challenges are as big or as small as you see them to be. Your point of view defines the size of your mountain. Your faith defines the stature of the challenge.

It is a matter of perspective. It is a matter of faith.

When problems pile up like a mountain, seek God. When issues challenge you, confront them with faith, solutions, and action.

You have the seed of faith to overcome obstacles. You possess the power to unveil the unknown and the choice to unleash your potential.

Faith moves mountains, parts the Red Sea, and topples giants. However, faith requires you to look at the challenge and take small steps forward.

Faith is the act of the will to form bridges to your potential.

Faith is the act of the mind to focus on challenges at hand.

Faith is the act of the heart to align hopes and dreams to your destiny.

Faith turns rocks of circumstances into verdant pastures.

Faith is placed in you. However, faith has to be planted. Like a small seed, allow faith to grow to a towering stature.

Let faith put a net of security around your dreams, aspirations, and life.

Let faith move you to take another step forward. In the end, small steps, small victories, and even defeats strung together shape your life.

"Now faith is the substance of things hoped for, the evidence of things not seen" (Heb. 11:1).

Faith is not a cosmic experience to a select few. We all have faith. You have faith.

Faith is not cryptic or hidden.

H. C. Villanueva

Faith is vibrant in the mind, real in the heart, and alive in the soul.

Faith is the key to open the gate of heaven and the door of your soul.

Faith helps you see diamonds in heaps of coals.

Faith helps you feel love in the midst of hate.

Faith helps you grab hope beyond the curtain of adversity

Faith ignites your soul like a sparkplug and triggers your mind to action.

Faith gives you hope. Faith gives you life. Faith gives you something to hold onto.

Let faith connect you to God, for God knows what is ahead.

The greatest display of faith is not parting the Red Sea, slaying giants, or making the earth stand still.

The greatest show of faith occurs when a soul commits to God, the Creator and Spotter of life.

View from the top

In auto racing, a spotter watches the race from a higher view.

The spotter becomes the extra eyes for the driver below on the racetrack.

Ralph Dale Earnhardt, Sr., was legendary in auto racing. He had a spotter.[1]

Dale Earnhardt was no stranger to the Daytona racetrack. For many years, he won numerous Daytona races. On the same speedway, he won Gatorade Twin 125s, Budweiser Shootouts, Pepsi 400s, and IROC races. Of the Gatorade Twin 125s wins, he connected many victories in a row from 1990 through 1999. On the other hand, during his twentieth attempt at the Daytona 500, he captured the checkered victory flag in 1998.

Three years later, a drastic event happened. During the final lap of the 2001 Daytona 500, this legendary driver faced the ultimate reality.

The final moments of his life unfolded at the 499th mile of the 500-mile race.

The finish line was in sight. At the final turn, he lost control of his race car and crashed. Moments later, he died.

This tragedy shows the frailty of life. This tragedy shows that no one knows when death will come knocking.

Death is not an end to the soul; it is only a threshold to eternity. Physical death is the moment when the spirit separates from the body. Spiritual death occurs when a soul is separated from God.

You do not have control over when you will physically die. However, you do have control when you will spiritually live or die.

"He who overcomes shall inherit all things, and I will be his God and he shall be My son. But the cowardly, unbelieving, abominable, murderers, sexually immoral, sorcerers, idolaters, and all liars shall have their part in the lake which burns with fire and brimstone, which is the second death" (Rev. 21:7. 8).

Between your first and final breath, you are given a life, you are given a choice, and you are given a chance to make something of it.

You are placed on earth to make a difference. I pray that you plant dreams in the garden of life and nurture ideas to grow towering forests of love, so others may enjoy the shades of your goodness.

QUESTIONS TO SEARCH YOUR SOUL

A. Do you have a spotter in life?

Find three spotters to provide life viewpoints.
Talk to your spotters at least once a month.
Give them permission to share truths about you.

B. Daily life: *Unleash the Beauty and Power of Love* to your friends

Create a nurturing place with friends.
Help friends grow in stature and faith.
Ask them to check your goals every month.

C. Self-discovery

Stretch your faith.
Enlarge the scope of life. Learn new things each day.
Get out of your comfort zone to do good deed.

28

Follow the Master

*A life without direction is pointless. A life without
love is empty. A life without God is dead.*

I traveled thousands of miles.

The summer heat parched my skin. The metal dog tag
dangling around my neck seared my flesh. At first, the heat was
unbearable--the hot air burned my lungs and the bright sun
blurred my vision. At the same time, a man with a "Smokey the
Bear" hat yelled inches from my ear.

At first, basic training was overwhelming. It was an inferno
of endless pestering. No little detail escaped the trainers. Drill
sergeants barked like pit bulls. However, behind these seemingly
torturous ordeals, there was a much bigger purpose.

Boot camp offered a structured place to develop character,
teamwork, and perseverance. Repetition of tasks helped us excel.
Regimented routines molded us into soldiers.

Basic training prepared us to face the greatest enemy. This
enemy is not out there on the battlefield but resides within.
Cowardice, pride, arrogance, and ignorance roar loudly in the

soul. The drill sergeants' job was to defeat the enemy within. As we overcome the war in the soul, the enemy outside is no match for a disciplined, well-trained, and well-equipped soldier.

Alarm bell

During the first morning, the drill sergeant threw a garbage can on the floor.

In the early morning stillness, the garbage can boomed like a cannon. The bang catapulted us out of our bunks like cannonballs.

Then, he pounded the garbage can like a maniac. The deafening sound quickened us and created chaos.

This 5 am alarm clock started the day. At first, we moved around like confused chickens running around. However, the drill sergeant turned on the light and gave us instructions to prepare for physical training (PT).

The first PT was hard. We ran couple of miles. The drill sergeants pushed us to exhaustion. We grasped for breath. I was in a daze and mucus oozed from my mouth.

During the first week, I was singled out. I was slow and had extra pounds. As a result, I was assigned to remedial PT. At 6 pm, I went to the race track, met the drill sergeant, ran two miles, and did more sit ups and pushups.

Before each meal, the drill sergeant ordered me in front leaning position, where only my two palms and shoes touched the ground and was left alone outside as the drill sergeant allowed other trainees enter the cafeteria. The time alone seemed like hours. Ten minutes later, the drill sergeant summoned me to join the group to eat.

I was turned into a spectacle. Sometimes, the drill sergeant ordered me to a dying cockroach position in front of the group. I lay flat on my back, and then raised my legs and arms straight up.

These ordeals were defining moments of my basic training.

The drill sergeant gave reasons why he was doing this to me.

For eight weeks, the drill sergeant was my mentor. He deflated my ego and murdered my untamed pride. He took time to help me pass the rigors of basic training.

Years later, I came to appreciate my drill sergeant. Maybe he knew about Hebrews 12:11: *"Now no chastening seem to be joyful for the present, but painful; nevertheless, afterward it yields the peaceable fruit of righteousness to those who have been trained by it."*

I was grateful for the extra help, spectacle, and encouragement. The extra training developed my character, strengthened my body, and turned me into a soldier.

Good habits

Before you face the world each day, pause.

Give some thought to what you are becoming. Each day, search your soul.

Each day, move your dreams, mold your character, and make your essence grow. Take one step closer to your purpose. *"Draw near to God and He will draw near to you. Cleanse your hands, you sinners; and purify your hearts, you double-minded"* (James. 4:8).

Find people to help you grow. Uncover their courage, moral fortitude, and unbending perseverance. Unveil their strengths and weaknesses.

Seek mentors. Learn from those who went before you. They give seasoned advice and offer priceless wisdom.

Seek coaches to guide you. They tell the truth about you that you may not want to hear. At the same time, they help you carve good habits to help you move beyond the horizon of faith.

QUESTIONS TO SEARCH YOUR SOUL

A. What are three areas of your life needing improvement?

Write them down.
Take time each day to find solutions.
Do simple things to improve your life.

B. Daily life: *Unleash the Beauty and Power of Love* to your neighbors

Create a nurturing place for your neighbors.
Ask friends to give unbiased observations about you.
Seek mentors to provide seasoned advice.

C. Self-discovery

Follow the examples of Christ.
Seek God for guidance.
Then, follow a path paved by God.

29

Countless Average

Defeat humbles the will. Failure builds character.
Perseverance propels the soul above the challenges.

The face looks puffy.

The thick rough skin encased a precious soul. Words slurped and saliva dripped from his lip.

From a distance, he looked normal. However, if you looked closer, you could see a person living an extraordinary life. He was different because he had Down's syndrome.

His name was Bob.[1]

I met him at a health spa.

Bob possessed the zest to live.

Bob's life was a beauty to behold. He had a simple curiosity about life. He did not have flashy dreams. However, he was curious about people. He helped others and greeted everyone crossing his path.

The past did not bother him. The future did not distract him. He lived in the moment. His eyes focused on tasks at hand.

One day, Bob had pneumonia and was admitted to a hospital.

Days later, he was in a coma and hooked to a respirator.

For a few days, Bob fought for his life. The vibrant life slipped away before our eyes.

At the funeral, hundreds came. People cried. All felt the loss. Many opened their hearts and shared gems from their soul. These gems were polished by Bob.

The memory of Bob sweetened saddened hearts.

Bob lived an average life but impacted us in an extraordinary way.

Marathon of life

I stood at the six-mile mark, on Ogden Street and Main Street, to watch the 2nd Annual Las Vegas Marathon. The chilly 51° F December morning welcomed runners from around the world.

The race started at 6 am.

After twenty-five minutes, elite runners passed by. They were splendors to see. They ran like thoroughbreds racing toward the finish line. They glided through the streets with no wasted motions. They leaned forward and looked toward the horizon.

Ten minutes later, different runners pounded the pavement. These runners were serious, but ran leisurely. Excess garb added flair, but slowed down these runners. However, they enjoyed themselves.

The 2nd Annual Las Vegas Marathon was no different from other races.

Over fifteen thousand runners took part. Forty-two nations were represented.

All participants wanted to finish the race.

This marathon was a drama to behold. The Elvis group, with forty runners, added glitz to the event.

Earlier during the week, a couple got married. During the race, the bridal group ran the 13.1-mile half-marathon. The bride and groom ran the grueling 26.2-mile course.

In addition, twenty sets of brides and grooms started the race. At the fifth mile, they went to a chapel, paused for a moment, confessed their vows, and finished the marathon.

Another couple captured the moment.

Twenty yards before the finish line, Matt got on his knees and proposed.

She said, "Yes!"

Mold life

The marathon of life is no different.

Each of us is given a chance to run the race called life.

Some are prepared. Some are not.

Some are building a life; some are simply existing.

Each runs a race in one's choosing. Some run to finish first at all costs. Others run just to finish the race.

You hold the power to choose how to run the race of life. You choose the path of the journey and you choose the pace.

"*Do you see a man who excels in his work? He will stand before kings; he will not stand before unknown men*" (Prov. 22:29).

The heart exposes itself when running the race. Defeat humbles the will, failure builds character, and perseverance propels the will above the challenges.

Each of us makes life unique to behold. God designed life with meaning and purpose.

You cannot fake happiness or fabricate love.

Do not chase love in depraved corners of society. Do not look for happiness in darkened halls of sin. Love is not out there or happiness is never far away.

Merriment stands closer than you think. Happiness resides within. It is an expression of a joyful soul. Happiness is a state of mind and a condition of the heart.

Love is mysterious, yet so real.

Life is real, yet so mysterious.

Finding love is an inner and outward journey. You do not know where love leads. However, you possess power to prepare your heart to grow love in the garden of life.

Love forms bridges to souls searching for joy, peace, and life. Also, love opens the curtain of eternity to unveil the saving grace of the Almighty.

As you journey, focus your eyes to see love at every turn. Train your mind to see blessings buried in heaps of pain. Expose the beauty of the soul when burdened with hurt, see possibilities when strained with struggles, and pluck pearls of joy from hardened anguish.

When you see light in darkness, you are ready to move forward. When you see hope in pain, you are ready to grow. When you find love in ashes of hate, you are ready to *Unleash the Beauty and Power of Love.*

Chapter 29: **Countless Average**

QUESTIONS TO SEARCH YOUR SOUL

A. What are your dreams?

Write your dreams down.
What are you doing about them?
Set aside four hours each week for polishing ideas,
dreams, and plans.

B. Daily life: *Unleash the Beauty and Power of Love* to your world

Create a nurturing place around you.
Meet the "Bobs" of this world.
Take time to know them.

C. Self-discovery

List your natural talents and skills.
Find ways to improve them.
Find ways to share your skills to help others.

30

Mom, You Are the Greatest

To Mom:
You brought me into this world with warmth and tenderness.
You nurtured me and you protected me when I was helpless.
When I was young, came home, and hurt my knees one day.
You smiled at me, dried my tears, and wiped the hurts away.

Mom you have planted morals and life's integrity within me.
I am grateful because they are a priceless compass guiding me.
Through the years you gave me valuable and practical advice.
Admonished me that wearing a miniskirt in public is not nice.

You sacrificed a great deal of yourself so better can I be.
Mom, I am thankful for the life, joy, love, and opportunity.
The journey through life is filled with wonders and adventures.
Your love and wisdom give me strength to face the future.

I am a young woman now. The earth waits for me to blossom.
You gave me wings to soar but forever held at your bosom.
There is a gentleman who is knocking at the door of my heart.
Mom, I need you to check him before my heart journey starts.

Love is filled with wonders, joy, hurt, and challenges every day.
Mom, you went though it all and I seek your advice along the way.
When it is time to have my own family I want to do my best.
Mom, you are my inspiration. MOM, You Are The Greatest.
Your Loving Daughter,

Part Seven

YOUR NEXT STEP

Part Seven: **Your Next Step**

CHECKLIST

Principles to instill

- Love was placed in your soul to feel, to grow, and to share.
- Love cannot be explained. Love has to be shared.
- Look inside. Something within is remarkable.

Things to do

- Spend soul-searching time as you watch sunsets.
- Share acts of kindness each day.
- Create a loving space for family, friends, and neighbors.

A life to build

- Give family members and friends a hug.
- Mail birthday cards even if their birthdays are months away.
- Volunteer to help people each month.

31

Unleash Life

*Life is real. The question is whether we
are real enough to face it.*

It was Friday the thirteenth.

The sky was shaded with clouds.

In the morning, gentle rain sprinkled on the leeward side of Oahu.[1] During the early afternoon, clouds covered the sky like cobblestones.

Stagnant air made the day dreary, gloomy, and balmy. However, sun rays pierced through the clouds like the glory of heaven reaching down to earth.

Over 2,500 miles away across the ocean, a woman autumn in years rushed to a post office. She hastened to mail a birthday card. The card was for me.

I was elated to have a kindred soul prompting me to value each moment of life. This tender cue inspired me to go on and helped me move forward to face another day, another year, another season.

At 5:24 pm, I received a call from Los Angeles. It was Ayko.[2]

Ayko's bubbling fervor ignited flickering gladness in me. Her kind spirit refreshed my soul.

Sadly, as she opened her heart, she shared a darker side of her life. After many years, she was fighting a life and death battle with cancer.

She tried hard to hide the struggle. She tried hard to contain the emotion. However, the pain gushed from the wall of her heart despite her valiant effort to remain upbeat.

She attempted to hold back the tears, but the pain from her soul began to drip on me. Her voice trembled as her soul anguished. I kept silent as she emptied the aches from her heart.

I paused for a moment.

I could not imagine she had paddled through a rough life. I did not sense that her life was bruised with pain.

Little did I know she lived in quiet agony as she battled life's storm.

However, I wondered, "Is she really left in a cold harsh world?" A woman in climactic years stood in the cold.

"The LORD is near to those who have a broken heart, and saves such as have a contrite spirit. Many are the afflictions of the righteous, but the LORD delivers him out of them all" (Ps. 34:18, 19).

A glorious day

The richness of her life echoed.

Two years earlier, Ayko came to Hawaii. While in Honolulu, she volunteered one Saturday each month to help the homeless.

She greeted volunteers with bold, hopeful words, "It is a glorious day!"

Ayko's optimism helped me see the brighter side of each event. She helped me see hope in the dark confines of life. She helped me see that simple moments, however mundane, are seeds to something beautiful.

Over six decades of living, precious truths grew in her soul. I pondered Ayko's motherly advice. She said, "Give everything to God. Give the little things you have. Let God work in you and through you." She reminded me of this verse, *"Humble yourselves in the sight of the Lord, and He will lift you up"* (James. 4:10).

She cheered people with an angelic smile.

The goodness of heaven shone through her, and a melody of kindness hummed in her soul. As a result, my life and others' lives were enriched.

As she continued to say, "It is a glorious day!" Great things await. Joy waits, beauty, and love wait to be unleashed.

She pressed forward trusting God. She, too, turned a new leaf, a new day, a new season. She marched forward changing the ashes of her life into something precious.

The days may be gloomy. However, beauty shines through her kind soul. Lives are changed because she shared from her heart precious gems polished by God.

Wondrous prism

"The heavens declare the glory of God; and the firmament shows His handiwork" (Ps. 19:1).

I often spend solemn moments watching the sun dip down the horizon. One late afternoon, it dawned on me. I now know why sunsets burst with colors--of yellow, orange, red, and spectacular scene.

Impurities rise and drift west. Dust floats up and diffuses the brightness of the setting sun. Gases and particles act as prism to expose the beauty wrapped in light. The sun turns reddish orange and gives a soft glow for a peaceful soul to enjoy.

When you pause, a sunset shows its grandeur. You enjoy the beauty of creation when the soul stops to appreciate the spectacular drama of nature.

Likewise, when you pause, you see life's splendor. When the soul slows down, things become clearer; something beautiful comes out from all life events, even the bad ones.

Failures, pains, and victories act as prisms to expose the beauty of life. During moments of laughter or in pain, joy prepares to burst forth from a grateful heart.

Pause for a moment. See the brilliance of creation and, at the same time, see the splendor of God within.

As you seek God, you see life more clearly. And as you seek life, you see more of God.

"If then you were raised with Christ, seek those things which are above, where Christ is, sitting at the right hand of God. Set your mind on things above, not on things on the earth. For you died, and your life is hidden with Christ in God" (Col. 3:1-3).

Life is real.

The question is whether we are real enough to face life.

Challenges are real. The question is whether we are real enough to face challenges.

There are many things God placed in the soul.

The measure of life is determined by God, not by what others say about you.

The depth of life is measured by how you have helped others, not by what was gathered.

The extent of life is gauged by what flows out from the soul, not by what was received.

When you give, good things happen.

The kindness you share comes back in good measure, plus a little bit more.

QUESTIONS TO SEARCH YOUR SOUL

A. What are your passions?

> What are the prisms in your life?
> Write them down.
> Find gems to be your life prisms.

B. Daily life: *Unleash the Beauty and Power of Love* to your family

> Create a loving place for family.
> Challenge each family member to excellence.
> Help people see obstacles as prisms through which to view goodness in all things.

C. Self-discovery

> Find your purpose and meaning in the Bible.
> Polish the rough gems within.
> Give family members room to grow.

32

Unleash Love

*Love is real. The question is whether we
are real enough to embrace love.*

It was a late Saturday afternoon.

We finished an outreach helping the homeless and started to
drive the cargo truck thirty miles back to town.

We stopped at a convenience store.

As we entered, a man said, "Sir, could you spare a dollar?"

My friend stopped next to the man, showed concern, and gave
the man his full attention.

My friend responded, "Sir, I cannot give you a dollar. This is
what I can do--I will go inside the store to buy you food."

The man relented with a twinkle in his eyes.

We went in and picked up bottled water and sandwiches. At
the counter, the manager tried to stop my friend from buying
sandwiches. She had overheard the conversation and tried to stop
us from helping the man.

The manager wanted the homeless man to move away from
the store so customers would not be badgered for money.

I looked at the manager's eyes and jokingly said, "Tomorrow is Sunday. My friend has to give an account to God for his deed today."

The manager smiled.

My friend returned to the man and gave him the sandwiches.

Veteran needs help

Weeks later, another event tugged my soul.

We stopped at an intersection. A man held a cardboard sign showing, "Veteran needs help!"

The man walked along the median of a busy highway. My friend opened the car window, summoned the man, and gave him a five-dollar bill.

I praised my friend for the good deed. However he said, "It is nothing. People need help from time to time. This is my moment to help."

At that moment, my eyes saw life showing its best. This act of kindness touched my soul. This simple gesture of goodness touched my heart.

I was reminded of these Bible verses: *"What does it profit, my brethren. if someone says he has faith but does not have works? Can faith save him? If a brother or sister is naked and destitute of daily food, and one of you say to them, 'Depart in peace, be warmed and filled,' but you do not give them the things which are needed for the body, what does it profit? Thus also faith by itself, if it does not have works, is dead"* (James 2:14-17).

With God, loving is not hard to do. It is simple.

Compassion does not cost much or compassion does not ask big things. Love asks simple faith and informal gestures of goodness.

Love cannot be reasoned or explained.

In order to feel its power, love has to be given. In order to feel its beauty, love must be shared.

It is in loving that hardened hearts soften; it is in loving that goodness grows within; and it is in loving that you find life.

Be a part of love when it is transforming. Be in it when it is growing and see love in its grandeur when it is blooming.

Love unlocks closed hearts. At the same time, love opens the windows of heaven. Sharing your life exposes what is inside. In the process, you discover who you are and unveil the meaning and purpose of life.

On the cross

On Calvary, Christ showed the ultimate act of love.

This scene provides a vivid picture of two people staring at their eternity.

Two criminals had choices.

One sneered at the Savior; the other welcomed His grace.

You will be confronted with the same question.

What are you doing with the love of Christ?

Here is the story:

"With Him they also crucified two robbers, one on His right and the other on His left" (Mark 15:27).

"Then one of the criminals who were hanged blasphemed Him, saying, 'If You are the Christ, save Yourself and us. But the other answering, rebuked him, saying, 'Do you not even fear God, seeing you are under the same condemnation? And we indeed justly, for we receive the due reward of our deeds; but this Man has done nothing wrong.' Then he said to Jesus, 'Lord, remember me when You come into Your kingdom.'

And Jesus said to him, 'Assuredly, I say to you, today you will be with Me in Paradise'" (Luke 23:39-43).

Demons tremble at the mention of His name.

Man uses His name in vain.

Some get offended when His name is voiced. Many despise Him; others embrace His grace.

People have a wide range of responses to the name of Jesus Christ. However, the most important viewpoint is yours. Other people's opinion will not matter when you are judged by God.

The love of Christ extends to all and drapes over mankind, even though we should have been the ones on the cross.

The extent of our relationship with Christ shapes our lives and determines our eternity.

Others have made their choices known.

How about you?

Chapter 32: **Unleash Love**

QUESTIONS TO SEARCH YOUR SOUL

A. What acts of kindness can you share this week?

Write them down.
Do them.
Then, share them with friends.

B. Daily life: *Unleash the Beauty and Power of Love* to your friends

Create a loving place for friends.
Ask a friend to go with you to give food to homeless people.
Nourish your friendships each day.

C. Self-discovery

Love is mysterious and elusive, but also confronting and open.
Each day, take time to share your life with others.
Each day, take time to know the face of love.

33

What Do You Have in Your Hands?

The fruit depends on what you planted. If you plant love, you harvest love. If you plant hate, you harvest hate. If you plant doubt, you harvest doubt. If you plant nothing, you get nothing, plus more problems.

A boy owned a slingshot.

In the hands of a young shepherd, the slingshot was a toy.

As the boy grew older, the slingshot became a tool and a weapon. He used it to protect the family's herd of sheep.

Then, opportunity knocked.

He was at the scene, but the offer was not given to him. He was a courier taking bread and cheese to his brothers on the battlefield. However, the young man heard the offer of the king.

The young man piqued with eagerness. So he asked a soldier to repeat the decree.

"So the men of Israel said, "Have you seen this man who has come up? Surely he has come up to defy Israel; and it shall be that the man who kills him the king will enrich with great riches, will give

him his daughter, and give his father's house exemption from taxes in Israel" (1 Sam. 17:25).

The challenge was extraordinary.

Goliath was huge and imposing. All feared his stature, except one--David.

"*Then David said to the Philistine, 'You come to me with a sword, with a spear, and with a javelin. But I come to you in the name of the LORD of hosts, . . .'"* (1 Sam. 17:45).

Faith brought David on the stage. One stone, one slingshot, one humble heart, and the power of God raised David to the next level.

Likewise, life is given to you. Life is in you to feel, to mold, and to share. You choose what grows in you, and you choose what comes out of your life. Opportunities are placed before you. It is up to you to plant your efforts and persevere to harvest the fruits of your undertaking.

The fruit of life depends on what was planted. If you plant love, you harvest love. If you plant hate, you harvest hate. If you plant doubt, you harvest doubt. If you plant nothing, you get nothing . . . plus more problems.

What do you have in your hands? What is in your heart?

What is in your soul?

It is more than you know.

On the balance

Armies camp on each side of the border.

Warriors posture for battle. War draws near and destruction is imminent.

This war involves enemies with no distinct faces, no uniforms, and no boundaries. This enemy hides in the cover of darkness, blends among the innocent, and comes out when no one suspects.

The greatest enemy lives around us. This enemy can live in us and needs to be brought into submission under the redemptive power of Jesus Christ.

The enemy is sin.

H. C. Villanueva

Sin blinds us to see who we are. Our self-absorption makes us greedy. Pride makes the soul happy for a short time, but wretched later.

During the coming years, history reveals the scale of what is at stake.

Urgent moments show our foolishness; however, history reveals our character. Also, urgent moments expose our character and history reveals our foolishness.

History provides lessons to teach us.

Now, similar events are happening again. Inaction creates more problems, ushers destruction, and brings more death.

What are we going to do with the challenge at hand?

Warriors falter in the presence of fools rather than in the battlefield battle. Warriors face cannons of criticism rather than swords of the enemy.

How short-sighted are we?

Danger knocks from every side. Yet, we cannot see beyond our cares and comfort. We have been sitting on the fence of opinions far too long.

Nobody stood up

In 1938, the Munich Pact was signed by Great Britain, France, Italy, and Hitler.

The prime minister of Great Britain coined the treaty as the "peace of our time" agreement.

From the 1920s to 1941, most Americans did not want to deal with conflicts brewing across the globe. Before December 7, 1941, World War I lingered in the minds of the American people. A strong isolationist view postured America away from conflicts emerging in Europe and Asia. The United States Congress passed neutrality laws preventing America from getting involved in faraway disputes. As a result, conflicts flared into a global bloodbath--World War II.

Before the "Day of Infamy," leaders wanted to discuss a peace agreement.[2] However, leaders were fooled to discuss peace while warships of destruction sailed toward Pearl Harbor.

Now, it happens again. Leaders are fooled again. We are fooled again. Vehicles of death are launched to destroy the world.

Where is the leadership?

During the coming years, we will choose leaders. These leaders are reflections of us. Therefore, we need to look at ourselves.

What kind of leaders are we electing?

In order to answer this question, ask, "What kind of people are we?"

As dangers lurk in our midst, do we elect leaders who subscribe to the "peace of our time" mentality? At every level, society needs leaders as bastions of hope to lift us out of complacency. The leader is all of us. The leader society needs is you.

To *Unleash the Beauty and Power of Love,* take the step to bring truth into the midst of darkness, share hope with those who have lost faith, and give love to those who are hurting.

Destructive events happen all around. However, the greatest calamity involves a life without hope, a soul without purpose, and a heart without love.

Something in us is powerful. God left tokens of His greatness, power, and love in all of us.

What do you have in you? What do you have in your hands?

It is much more than you know.

Chapter 33: **What Do You Have in Your Hands?**

QUESTIONS TO SEARCH YOUR SOUL

A. What do you have in your hands?

Write three things simmering within you.
What are your talents?
What are you doing about them today?

B. Daily life: *Unleash the Beauty and Power of Love* to your neighbors

Create a loving place for neighbors.
Share ideas to solve societal issues.
Commit a selfless act of kindness for a neighbor each week.

C. Self-discovery

You are given talents and skills.
What are they?
What are you doing with your skills and talents?

34

The Journey Continues

Life grows cold when you do not put ideas in the furnace of adversity. When you tarry, dreams become wavering titillations of the soul, and aspirations turn into useless trinkets of the mind.

This journey with me comes to an end.

Unleash the Beauty and Power of Love shares ideas to explore, truths to see, and paths upon which to walk.

As you spend quiet moments, you find truths, unearth life-changing principles, and learn about yourself. *"Trust in the LORD with all your heart, and lean not on your own understanding; in all your ways acknowledge Him, and He shall direct your paths"* (Prov. 3:5, 6).

Each day, engage your mind to find truths, channel your passion to an eternal cause, and go hard after life. With hope, go toward your dreams. With faith, take simple steps. With perseverance, press on. With God as your guide, your life moves closer to what you were meant to be.

Now, the spotlight shines on you.

You have endured failures of life, faced pains of the heart, and coped with anguish of the soul. However, there is much life ahead.

More pain, more hurt, and more failure await you. At the same time, more victories, more peace, and more love wait to be ushered in.

When dark clouds come, take heart. When you look toward the horizon after a rainstorm, a rainbow appears. If you wait long enough, pieces of coal under intense pressure turn into precious gems. By the same token, if you look hard enough after a struggle, pearls of joy glisten in heaps of pain.

During cloudy moments, pause. Look for rays of hope and get a clear view of God.

Walk a simple life and enjoy simple moments for they are building blocks of life.

Display a gentle smile, give encouragement, and share time to help others. When you offer plain gestures of love, you release lives from bondage of doubt, fear, and past.

Know this--life grows cold when you do not put ideas in the furnace of adversity. Dreams fade away when you do not visit them often. Plans become wishful thoughts when you do not put action behind them. When you tarry, dreams become wavering titillations of the soul and aspirations turn into useless trinkets in the mind.

The key . . .

This story portrays what many of us do with our lives.

A supervisor gave a key and a shovel to a laborer.

He said, "Here are your tools. The goal is to bring water to the next field half a mile away. Build a canal."

The manager left to tend other projects.

The laborer scratched his head and said, "This takes time and requires work."

H. C. Villanueva

Out of habit, because he had been shoveling dirt all his life, he took the shovel, placed the key in his pocket, and started to scoop dirt.

He took a break during lunch and continued to work until evening.

At the end of the day, every fiber in his arms screamed with pain. Back muscles ached. Dirt covered his arms and face. Sweat left dirt trails on both sides of his face. But he was happy to give a full day's work.

The supervisor came back. To his dismay, the laborer completed only five feet.

He said, "I gave you a key and a shovel. The key I gave you has a tag on it: Bulldozer One. The key belongs to a huge bulldozer. I know you have been shoveling dirt all of your working life. But recently, you were trained to operate bulldozers. The machine is parked fifty feet away. It is filled with fuel and ready to be used."

The laborer jumped on the machine and moved tons of dirt. The laborer made progress. Yet, the day ended without a canal and darkness entered the scene.

How is your canal project?

What are you doing with the keys or talents you have been given?

God waits

The apostle Paul wrote, *"Being confident of this very thing, that He who has begun a good work in you will complete it until the day of Jesus Christ"* (Phil. 1:6).

Say, *"Show me Your ways, O LORD; teach me Your paths. Lead me in Your truth and teach me, for You are the God of my salvation; on You I wait all the day"* (Ps. 25:4, 5).

Life is a journey of discovery.

Life is a journey of unfolding yourself and a journey of finding the love of God.

Step into life expecting to find grace from heaven along the way.

Go. Open the door. Enter into a life ordained by God. Now:

1. Have quiet moments each day to check your heart.

2. Find like-minded souls willing to grow with you.

3. Read the Bible every day. The Bible is the manual to life.

4. Share your dreams, do your plans, and plant your aspirations.

5. Be curious to learn new things. Find ways to improve your life.

6. Let God transform you and walk with God each step of the way.

7. Share love each day.

So what is the next step?

Continue to share love each day. Continue to discover the gift you have been given. And continue to draw closer to God.

Read the Bible every day. Ask friends to read this book with you. Help each other grow in truth and in Christ.

Learning is a vital, lifelong routine. Knowledge provides tools, truth helps you move forward, and wisdom makes you shine along the way.

"But the wisdom that is from above is first pure, the peaceable, gentle, willing to yield, full of mercy and good fruits, without partiality and without hypocrisy" (James 3:17).

Take a small step. That little step begins something amazing. Step out of your comfort zone and begin to trust God. Start with a simple action, a simple idea, or a simple step toward the challenge.

H. C. Villanueva

However pointless or trivial, small steps strung together create a journey. By the same token, small acts of kindness grouped together build an amazing life.

As life is set before you, grab the chance.

As each breath is given, make every effort have an eternal impact.

Start today,

Start now.

For me, my journey came together when I read the Bible with an eager heart.

Now, my passion is more focused and the journey is much sweeter.

Each day, I take baby steps.

Pieces of my life take shape with greater meaning. Dreams are watered with love, nourished with perseverance, and begin to show outward with grace. Yet, this is only the beginning of my journey and I have long ways to go.

So, my journey continues. Likewise, your journey continues. I pray you go through life with love. I pray you journey with God, for He can show the way.

Drama continues

Life presents the greatest drama you will ever see.

Do not miss the life unfolding on the stage. Do not miss the life unfolding in the darker confines of your life. At the same time, do not miss the love growing within.

One of life's missions involves praising God.

The other calling summons you to be a messenger of hope to rescue souls sinking in despair.

Each day let this be your prayer: *"You are worthy, O Lord, to receive glory and honor and power; for You created all things, and by Your will they exist and were created"* (Rev. 4:11).

You find love when you give your life to Jesus Christ. Christ guides you to live, shows you how to love, and helps you *Unleash the Beauty and Power of Love*.

At the end of your days, I pray you will be able to say, *"I have fought the good fight, I have finished the race, I have kept the faith"* (2 Tim. 4:7).

Have a God-ordained journey.

Get in the arena. Step on the stage.

Have a great drama.

Enjoy your life.

QUESTIONS TO SEARCH YOUR SOUL

A. What is your next step?

Memorize 1 Corinthians 13.

Find people willing to grow with you in Christ.

Tell friends about your dreams and ask them to check on you each month.

B. Daily life: *Unleash the Beauty and Power of Love* to your world

Create a loving place around you.

Do something good each day.

Find a church or group and volunteer to help others in need.

C. Self-discovery

So what is the next step?

Set a four-hour appointment with yourself every week.

Use this time to get in tune with God.

35

Just Me, the Voice Crying Within
IV

You are now standing before Almighty God
to judge your acts when you were carefree.

You have no voice, you have no influence,
all is silence; the time is now to judge thee.

This story had a sad ending and millions
follow this old, beaten, well used road.

You were young, lively, and full of dreams
without worry, without care, and big as a toad.

Do not ignore me, I am your friend, I am your
inner conscience, I am your spirit given by God.

I am the essence of your life and you need
me to *Unleash the Beauty and Power of Love.*

Appendix I
Your Greatest Confession

The greatest commandment
"'And you shall love the LORD your God with all your heart, with all your soul, with all your mind, and with all your strength.' This is the first commandment. And the second like it, is this: 'You shall love your neighbor as yourself.' There is no other commandment greater than these" (Mark 12:30-31).

The greatest realization
"Father, I have sinned against heaven and before You" (Luke 15:18b).

The greatest invitation
"Behold, I stand at the door and knock. If anyone hears My voice and opens the door, I will come in to him and dine with him, and he with Me" (Rev. 3:20).

The greatest promise
"If we confess our sins, He is faithful and just to forgive us our sins and to cleanse us from all unrighteousness" (1 John 1:9).

The greatest love
"For God so loved the world that He gave His only begotten Son, that whoever believes in Him should not perish but have everlasting life" (John 3:16).

Your greatest confession
Dear Jesus, come into my life and be my Savior and Lord. Please forgive me, cleanse me, and help me. Come into my life Amen.

Appendix II

The Greatest of These Is . . .

1 Corinthians 13

1. *Though I speak with the tongues of men and of angels, but have not love, I have become sounding brass or a clanging cymbal.*
2. *And though I have the gift of prophecy, and understand all mysteries and all knowledge, and though I have all faith, so that I could remove mountains, but have not love. I am nothing.*
3. *And though I bestow all my good to feed the poor, and though I give my body to be burned, but have not love, it profits me nothing.*
4. *Love suffers long and is kind; love does not envy; love does not parade itself, is not puffed up;*
5. *Does not behave rudely, does not seek its own, is not provoked, thinks no evil;*
6. *Does not rejoice in iniquity, but rejoices in the truth;*
7. *Bears all things, believes all things, hopes all things, endures all things.*
8. *Love never fails. But whether there are prophecies, they will fail, whether there are tongues, they will cease, whether there is knowledge, it will vanish away.*
9. *For we know in part and we prophesy in part.*
10. *But when that which is perfect has come, then that which is in part will be done away.*
11. *When I was a child, I spoke as a child, I understood as a child; I though as a child, but when I became a man, I put away childish things.*
12. *For now we see in a mirror, dimly, but then face to face. Now I know in part, but then I shall know just as I also am known.*
13. *And now abide faith, hope, love, these three; but the greatest of these is love.*

Appendix III

Love is ...

1. Love suffers long. (Love is patient.)

2. Love is kind.

3. Love does not _____.

4. Love does not parade_____.

5. Love is not puffed _____

6. Love does not behave _____.

7. Love does not seek its _____.

8. Love is not _____.

9. Love thinks no _____.

10. Love does not rejoice in _____.

11. Love rejoices in the _____.

12. Love bears all _____.

13. Love believes all_____.

14. Love endures all _____.

15. Love never fails. God never fails.

Appendix IV

Share Your Journey

You have a unique journey. You have a distinct life to impart.
Share your story with your family, friends, and neighbors. Let also
us hear your story as well.

To share your story, write to:

H. C. Villanueva
PO BOX 30785
Honolulu, HI 96820
USA

Notes

INTRODUCTION

1. Guidebook: 2 Tim. 3:16-17; measuring stick: Heb. 4:11-13; lamp: Ps. 119:105.

2. John 5:39, *"You search the scriptures..."*

CHAPTER 2

1. Actual name changed.

CHAPTER 3

1. This story is first heard in a sermon by Pastor Paul Yonggi Cho, Yoido Full Gospel Church, Seoul, South Korea, circa 1990. Koreans who crossed the border to South Korea have given similar accounts. The author took the liberty of adding dialogue to the story.

CHAPTER 6

1. This story is a fusion of five people who found Christ in the midst of struggle. I am one of them. I endured barrages of criticisms when I was young. It took the saving grace of Christ, the power of the Holy Spirit, and the Word of God to bring me to the rightful mind God intended.

CHAPTER 7

1. Actual name changed.

CHAPTER 9

1. The Iolani Palace is a historic building where Hawaiian royalty once lived.

CHAPTER 13

1. *Aloha*: means "welcome" or "hello" when greeting someone, or "goodbye" when parting. From the 2006 season: Humanitarian Bowl: Nevada 20 vs. Miami 21. Sheraton Hawaii Bowl: Hawaii 41 vs. Arizona State 24.

CHAPTER 16

1. Source: Raytheon Company: Our Company>History>Technology Leadership, http://www. raytheon.com (Copyright © 2008-2011).

CHAPTER 17

1. Matt. 5:13, *"You are the salt of the earth; but if the salt loses its flavor, how shall it be seasoned? It is then good for nothing but to be thrown out and trampled underfoot by me."*

2. Numbers 24-25

CHAPTER 18

1. Rick Green, *Freedom's Frame,* Revolutionary Strategies, 2008, Page 71-72 quoting John Adams' letter to Abigail Adams dated September 16, 1774.

2. John Hancock signed the Declaration of Independence on July 4, 1776. He was the president of the Continental Congress. Other signers signed later.

3. This chapter was added to affirm that your life is a seed to be planted in society. Also, your heart is a field upon which the nation will be built. The cumulative nature of our souls determines the stature of our nation.

CHAPTER 23

1. Actual name changed.

CHAPTER 26

1. John F. Love, *McDonald's: Behind the Arches.* New York City: Random House Publishing Group, 1995.

CHAPTER 27

1. Leigh Montville, *At the Altar of Speed*, New York City: Doubleday, 2001.

CHAPTER 29

1. Actual name changed.

CHAPTER 31

1. Oahu is the third largest in the chain of 117 Hawaiian islands. It contains about 70 percent of Hawaii's population of 1.3 million.

2. Actual name changed.

CHAPTER 33

1. 1 Samuel 17: David and Goliath.

2. "Day of Infamy": Coined by President Roosevelt in a joint session of Congress on December 8, 1941.

Acknowledgments

I thank my accountability group members--Glenn and others who came to the meetings for a season. You provided life lessons and allowed me to see the wonders of your lives unfold as you follow Jesus Christ.

I thank the Kailua writers group. I thank you for allowing me to see your humility, teachable hearts, and perseverance.

I thank you Stephen Escher and Sara Wood, editors. You are heaven-sent.

I extend my appreciation to YOU. You now hold this book. You invested in this book or someone was gracious to share this book with you.

Open your soul and see what is inside. Share life lessons. Give encouragement to people around you. Love yourself, family, friends, neighbors, and most of all love God.

About the author

H. C. Villanueva is a graduate from the University of Hawaii with BBA in management. He lives and works in Honolulu, Hawaii. He enjoys the Hawaiian outdoors and likes solemn outdoor scenes to take the soul to quiet solitude.